CLASSROOM DATA TRACKING

Data-Tracking Tools at Your Fingertips!

Grade 1

D1609064

Carson-Dellosa Publishing, LLC
PO Box 35665
Greensboro, NC 27425 USA
carsondellosa.com

978-1-4838-3439-9
01-158161151

Table of Contents

Math

Language Arts

What Is Classroom Data Tracking?

Being able to prove student growth is more important than ever, making classroom data tracking essential in today's classroom. Data tracking is capturing student learning through both formative and summative assessments and displaying the results. Further assessment of the results can then become an active part of teaching, planning, and remediation. Because teachers are accountable to families and administrators, and time is always at a premium in the classroom, using a simple yet comprehensive data-tracking system is a must.

This book will help make this important data-collection task manageable. The data-tracking tools—charts, rubrics, logs, checklists, inventories, etc.—are easy to use and modifiable to fit any classroom. The tools will help you collect quantitative and qualitative information on each student's level of mastery in any part of your curriculum. Having specific details at your fingertips will aid in setting goals with students, keeping families informed, updating administrators, and displaying progress at student conferences.

An important component of good classroom data tracking is involving students in their own progress so that they can take ownership of their learning. Statistics prove that when students monitor their own learning and track their own growth, they are more highly motivated and perform better. In addition, a good data-tracking system presents avenues for celebrating student successes. Such opportunities are presented here, whether with an "I've done it!" check box or a rating score, and serve to create the intrinsic motivation we all want to see in students.

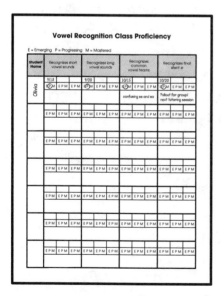 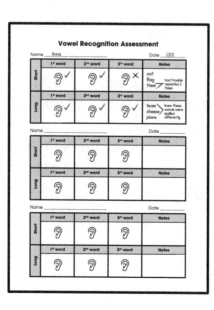 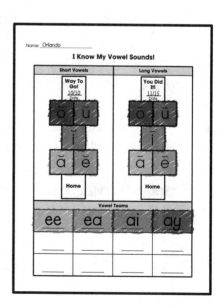

Completed data-tracking sheets for vowel sounds

Why Should I Use Data Tracking?

Teachers are busy and do not need new tasks, but data tracking is a must because in today's data-driven classroom, information is crucial. Fortunately, classroom data tracking can be an at-your-disposal, invaluable tool in many ways:

- Data tracking creates a growth mindset. It shifts focus from a pass/fail mentality to one of showing growth over time.
- It allows you to see any gaps in concepts that need reteaching so that you can easily create focused remediation groups.
- It allows for more targeted lesson planning for the upcoming weeks. Pre-assessments can help you justify spending little to no time on skills that students have already mastered or more time on skills where students lack the expected baseline knowledge. Post-assessments can also help you determine whether students need more time or, if not, what topics you should address next.
- It provides you with daily information and allows you to give students feedback and guidance more regularly.
- It involves students with tracking their own data so that they can easily see their own progress.
- It gives students a sense of pride and ownership over their learning.
- It helps create data portfolios that are useful tools for families, administrators, and student conferences.

Data Tracking in Your Classroom

As standards become more rigorous, data tracking is becoming a necessary part of an already full daily classroom routine. The pages in this book are intended as tools that will help you manage your classroom data and create a customized system to make data tracking more manageable. This book is designed to allow you to choose the reproducibles that work specifically for you and your students. You may even choose to use some reproducibles only for certain groups of students instead of the entire class. This book also allows you to integrate assessments into your current routines by using informal observations and other formative assessments instead of interrupting the flow with traditional tests. If possible, try to involve students in tracking their own data by using reproducibles, graphs, and sample work to create and manage their own portfolios (for more detailed data-tracking management tips, see Managing Data Tracking on pages 8–9).

How to Use This Book

This book includes four main types of pages. Refer to the following sample pages and descriptions to help you get the most out of this resource.

Each anchor and domain section begins with a learning crosswalk. Use the crosswalk to help you better understand what students should know from the previous year and what they will need to know for the next year to better guide your plans for teaching, assessment, and remediation.

A concepts checklist follows the crosswalk for each anchor and domain. Use the checklist to track which concepts you have taught and when. Write the standard code (such as OA.A.1) in the top-left box and describe the concept in the large space. Use some or all of the boxes to the right to list the dates that you taught, tested, and retaught the concept. Make multiple copies as needed.

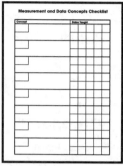

An explanation page precedes each set of three reproducibles. Use this page to learn about the intended use for each reproducible, to find additional suggestions for use, and to see an example of the reproducible in use.

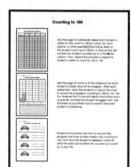

The type of reproducibles included for each concept will vary according to the types of reproducibles that are most useful for assessing that concept. Reproducibles may include whole-class recording sheets, conference sheets, open-ended assessment pages, or pages where students take charge of their own goals and learning. Use the explanation page before each set to better understand how to use each page.

In addition, use the Standards Assessed chart on page 10 to plan for and keep track of the standards and related assessments for a single subject at a glance. Simply record all of the standards for the subject, the dates taught, and any other brief notes you choose to record (assessment types, overall class proficiency, etc.).

Getting Started

You can start data tracking at any point in the school year. If you are new to data tracking, it may be helpful to start small with a single subject until you become more comfortable with the process. Use the following guidelines to help you start a data-tracking system in your classroom (for more detailed data-tracking management tips, see Managing Data Tracking on pages 8–9).

1. Choose the best format for your classroom.
You may choose to have a single binder to collect data or have individual student binders or folders (for more information, see Which Format Is Best? on page 7).

2. Add a cover page.
Because the data-tracking binder will play a starring role in your school year, design an attractive cover that will make the binder identifiable and enjoyable to use. If students are also creating binders or folders, have them add cover pages as well.

3. Organize the binder(s) into sections.
Decide what subjects and topics you will be assessing and use tabs or dividers to clearly divide and label them.

4. Choose a rating system.
Although you may use different systems depending on what and how you will be assessing, use a single rating system for the majority of assessments to create consistency, cohesiveness, and clarity.

Use the following guidelines to help you set a clear tone for the year if using student binders as well.

5. Compose guidelines or a "mission statement."
Guidelines or a short "mission statement" will let students know what is expected of them and make them accountable with their data tracking. If desired, have students keep copies at the beginning of their notebooks and have both students and family members sign them at the beginning of the school year.

6. Have students set long-term and short-term goals.
Long-term goals will give students targets to work toward. Short-term goals will give students attainable checkpoints along the way. It may also be helpful to give students standards checklists in student-friendly language and to have students keep written goals in their binders as reminders.

Other Suggestions

Here are some additional important elements to consider before beginning a data-tracking system:

- *How to recognize students for their successes throughout the year.* Consider ideas such as placing stars programmed with students' names on a Reaching for the Stars bulletin board, giving special rewards, or giving verbal recognition along with a unique class cheer.

- *How to include families in this endeavor.* It can be as simple as sending letters home at the beginning of the year, having student-led conferences using the data binders, or sharing goals with families so that students can work on their goals at home as well.

- *How to maintain student binders.* It may be helpful to provide students with rubrics at the beginning of the year, outlining the expectations for maintaining and assessing their binders periodically to make sure that they continue to include samples and keep the binders neat and organized.

- *How to store student binders.* Decide where to keep the binders—at students' desks or in a separate location. If keeping them in a separate location, you may need to set guidelines for when students can access and add to them.

Which Format Is Best?

Because classroom data-tracking systems need to last for an entire year, many teachers create and maintain them in three-ring binders because of their durability. However, you may choose to keep student work in folders if space is an issue or if students will be storing less information.

A Single Teacher Binder	A Teacher Binder and Student Binders
Pros • Convenient format means the information can always be with you. • You can store all of the information in one place.	**Pros** • Students can move sample work with them each year. • You can include more information because space is not limited. • You have less to do when preparing for conferences.
Cons • You have to gather student work when preparing for conferences. • Space is limited.	**Cons** • It can be time-consuming to work with numerous binders. • It can be challenging to assess class proficiency when sample work is in individual binders.

Managing Data Tracking

Managing the Teacher Binder

- Choose a durable two- or three-inch binder to store all of the important information for the whole year.

- Use the teacher binder as the one place to store the following important assessment-related tools and reproducibles:
  - a copy of the standards at the front of your binder for easy reference
  - copies of the resources and assessment tools for your grade, such as pacing guides, word lists, fluency tests, and reading level charts
  - master copies of assessments (You may also choose to store these separately for space reasons.)

- Consider separating the binder into two sections—overall class proficiency and individual student data. In the class proficiency section, keep information such as what standards you taught when, overall class scores, and student grouping information. Use the individual student section to store running records, baseline tests, remediation forms, and anecdotal notes.

- At the beginning of the school year, assign students numbers and use a set of numbered tabs to organize individual student data in a single place. Add a copy of student names and assigned numbers to the front of the individual data section.

Managing Student Binders

- Consider copying yearlong tracking sheets on card stock instead of copy paper for durability.

- Color code sections to make it easier for students to quickly find the correct pages. For example, copy all sight word pages on yellow paper.

- For younger students, have volunteers preassemble the binders. Include all of the tracking sheets for the year (even if you won't use some until later) to avoid having to add pages later.

- Provide students with several three-hole-punched page protectors for storing sample work, which is often not prepunched.

- Devote a short, designated time each week to allow students to add sample work to and organize their binders.

Tips and Tricks

Organize everything.
- Use file folders to create dividing tabs in a binder. Cut off the half of a file folder with the tab, three-hole punch it, and place it in your binder.
- Keep binders simple by using one pocket for each subject.

Save time.
- Use pens in different colors to make recording dates on a recording sheet simpler. Instead of writing the same date numerous times, simply write the date once in one color and record all of the data from that day using that color. If adding data from another date, repeat with a different color.
- Choose a standard proficiency scale and use it consistently throughout the binder. For example,

E, P, M (emerging, progressing, mastered)	NS, B, OL, A (not seen, beginning, on level, above)
✓-, ✓, ✓+	–, +, ++
a 0–4 rubric	your own unique system

Fit assessment into your day.
- Keep sheets of large labels (such as 2" × 4") on a clipboard. Carry the clipboard throughout the day and use the labels to record any informal observations about individual students. Record each student's name, the date, and your observation on a label. At the end of the day, simply place the label in the corresponding student's section.
- Use your weekly or monthly plan to copy the relevant whole-class progress charts and conference sheets ahead of time. Keep them on a clipboard so that they are at hand when observing students throughout the week or month.
- Focus on assessing or observing only three to five students per day.

Make the reproducibles work for your classroom.
- Add text before copying to create a unique assessment.
- Add, remove, or alter items such as write-on lines or date lines.
- Use a different scale than suggested (see the table above for ideas).
- Use pencil when recording on whole-class checklists so that it is simple to change marks as students progress.
- Use highlighters to draw attention to skills that need remediation, to an individual student's areas of need, or to create targeted small groups.
- Highlight or add stickers beside student goals on graphs and other tracking sheets to give students something visible to work toward.

Standards Assessed

Subject _____ **Quarter** _____

Standard/Topic	Date	Date	Date	Date	Notes

Name: _____   Date: _____

Math Skills Inventory

Numbers and Operations in Base Ten

Counts forward from
☐ 25   ☐ 50   ☐ 75   ☐ 100

Skip counts
☐ 5s   ☐ 10s

Addition
☐ adds one-digit numbers within 100
☐ adds two-digit numbers
☐ adds 10 mentally
☐ adds three numbers

Subtraction
☐ subtracts multiples of 10
☐ subtracts 10 mentally

Numbers to 120
☐ reads number to 120
☐ writes numbers to 120
☐ models numbers to 120

Uses strategies
☐ addition
☐ subtraction

Compares
☐ one-digit numbers
☐ two-digit numbers

Understands place value
☐ ones   ☐ tens

Operations and Algebraic Thinking

☐ adds fluently within 10
☐ subtracts fluently within 10
☐ adds and subtracts within 20
☐ solves word problems

Understands math symbols
☐ +   ☐ −   ☐ =

Finds
☐ missing addends
☐ unknown numbers

Measurement and Data

☐ orders three objects by length
☐ measures with nonstandard units

Tells time to the nearest
☐ hour   ☐ half-hour

Data
☐ organizes
☐ represents
☐ analyzes

Geometry

Recognizes and creates
☐ 2-D shapes   ☐ 3-D shapes

Partitions shapes equally into
☐ halves   ☐ fourths

Names
☐ halves   ☐ fourths

Name: _____   Date: _____

Language Arts Skills Inventory

Reading Level _____

Reading: Literature

Comprehension
- ☐ Asks and answers questions
- ☐ Understands key details

Story Elements
- ☐ Characters
- ☐ Setting
- ☐ Main events
- ☐ Understands story structure
- ☐ Recounts stories

Reading: Foundations

- ☐ Understands organization of books and print
- ☐ Identifies syllables in words
- ☐ Distinguishes between long/short vowels
- ☐ Identifies long vowel sounds
- ☐ Identifies short vowel sounds
- ☐ Identifies *y* and silent *e* sounds
- ☐ Knows common consonant digraphs

Identifies vowel teams

☐ ai	☐ ay	☐ ea	☐ ee
☐ igh	☐ ow	☐ oa	☐ ew
☐ ue	☐ ui	☐ ____	☐ ____

Fluency Level _____

Reading: Informational Text

- ☐ Tells main idea/topic
- ☐ Knows text type
- ☐ Knows text features
- ☐ Knows author's purpose

Speaking and Listening

- ☐ Participates appropriately in conversations with others

Writing

- ☐ Opinion ☐ Narrative ☐ Informative
- ☐ Edits
- ☐ Revises

Language

Single sentences
- ☐ produces ☐ expands

Can identify and use

☐ nouns	☐ plural nouns
☐ pronouns	☐ adjectives
☐ verbs	☐ prepositions

- ☐ Uses conventional spelling
- ☐ Uses capitals
- ☐ Uses punctuation
- ☐ Uses strategies to figure out unknown words
- ☐ Sorts and defines words by categories
- ☐ Identifies real-life connections between words

Operations and Algebraic Thinking
Standards Crosswalk

Kindergarten

Understand addition as putting together and adding to, and understand subtraction as taking apart and taking from.

- Represent and express addition and subtraction with various methods.
- Use addition and subtraction within 10 to solve word problems.
- Decompose numbers 1–10 into pairs in more than one way.
- Find the number that makes 10 when added to a given number.
- Fluently add and subtract within 5.

Understand and apply properties of operations and the relationship between addition and subtraction.

- Apply properties of operations as strategies to add and subtract.
- Understand subtraction as an unknown-addend problem.

Add and subtract within 20.

- Relate counting to addition and subtraction.
- Use strategies to add and subtract within 20.
- Demonstrate fluency with addition and subtraction within 10.

Work with addition and subtraction equations.

- Understand the meaning of the equal sign.
- Determine whether addition and subtraction equations are true or false.
- Find the unknown number in addition and subtraction equations.

Second Grade

Represent and solve problems involving addition and subtraction.

- Use addition and subtraction within 100 to solve one- and two-step word problems with unknowns in all positions (including those represented by a symbol).

Add and subtract within 20.

- Fluently add and subtract within 20 using mental strategies.
- Memorize all sums of two one-digit numbers.

Work with equal groups of objects to gain foundations for multiplication.

- Determine whether a group of up to 20 objects represents an odd or even number.
- Use addition to find the total number of objects arranged in rectangular arrays with up to five rows and up to five columns.
- Write an equation to express the sum of an array.

Operations and Algebraic Thinking
Concepts Checklist

Concept		Dates Taught				

Addition and Subtraction Word Problems

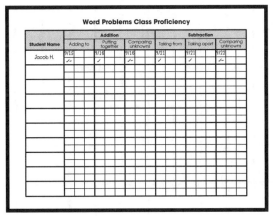

This page is ideal for keeping a record of your entire class's proficiency with the different types of word problems. Record student names in the left-hand column. As specific types of word problems are presented, record the date and use a check mark rating system to indicate progress of each student's ability to solve the word problems.

Use this page to observe individual students during an independent math assignment or a guided math group. Record the student's name, the date, the task assigned, and any addition or subtraction strategies you observe the student using. Use the *Notes* section to record strengths and areas to improve on as well as specific observations. If desired, print this page on adhesive label sheets to keep on a clipboard (visit our website for a free downloadable template). This makes conferencing and moving logs to student folders quick and easy.

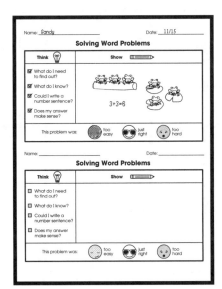

This checklist and self-assessment page is ideal for helping students think about the process of solving word problems. Give each student a word problem to solve. The word problem(s) can be clipped to this page or printed on an adhesive label and attached to the back of the page. Have students use the checklist on the left to work through the problem. On the right-hand side, the student should show his work to explain how he solved the problem. Finally, have him color or circle a face to show how he felt about the problem.

Word Problems Class Proficiency

Student Name	Addition			Subtraction		
	Adding to	Putting together	Comparing unknowns	Taking from	Taking apart	Comparing unknowns

Observation Sheet

Name _____ Date _____

Task observed _____

Strategies used _____

_____

Notes _____

_____

_____

_____

_____

_____

_____

Name _____ Date _____

Task observed _____

Strategies used _____

_____

Notes _____

_____

_____

_____

_____

_____

_____

Name _____ Date _____

Task observed _____

Strategies used _____

_____

Notes _____

_____

_____

_____

_____

_____

Name _____ Date _____

Task observed _____

Strategies used _____

_____

Notes _____

_____

_____

_____

_____

_____

Name: _____ Date: _____

Solving Word Problems

Think 💡	Show ✏️
☐ What do I need to find out? ☐ What do I know? ☐ Could I write a number sentence? ☐ Does my answer make sense?	

This problem was: 😌 too easy   😎 just right   😮 too hard

Name: _____ Date: _____

Solving Word Problems

Think 💡	Show ✏️
☐ What do I need to find out? ☐ What do I know? ☐ Could I write a number sentence? ☐ Does my answer make sense?	

This problem was: 😌 too easy   😎 just right   😮 too hard

Addition and Subtraction within 20

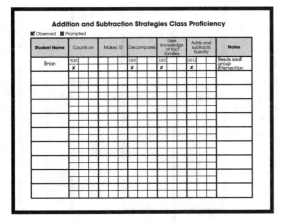

This page is perfect for tracking each student's progress in mastering addition and subtraction within 20. Record student names in the left-hand column. In the remaining columns, enter the date assessed and a level of mastery for each concept (note the scoring marks at the top of the page). Use the *Notes* section to record any observations or concerns. This page allows you to see at a glance which students have mastered these skills and which need help.

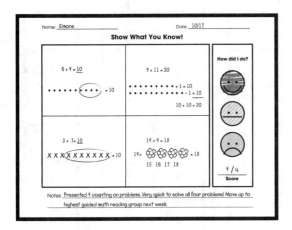

After you have introduced an addition and/or subtraction concept, have students use this page to show you what they know. Meet with students one-on-one or in a small group. Present four problems for the student to solve. As the student solves a problem, observe any strategies she used in solving it. Record strengths, weaknesses, strategies, and how the problems were introduced (orally, written, etc.) in the *Notes* section. Record the student's score. The student should color a face to show how she felt she did on the assessment.

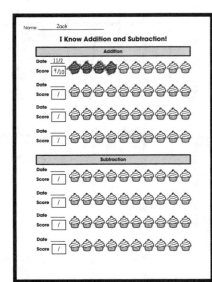

With this page, students can keep track of the progress they have made in learning how to add and subtract within 20. Present 10 problems for the student to solve. After the assessment, have him record the date and his score. To show his score, the student should color the amount of cupcakes for each problem he solved correctly. Use the top section for recording addition problems and the bottom section for recording subtraction problems. Insert this page in a student's portfolio to show the progression of addition and subtraction skills over time.

Addition and Subtraction Strategies Class Proficiency

☑ Observed ☒ Prompted

Student Name	Counts on			Makes 10			Decomposes			Uses knowledge of fact families			Adds and subtracts fluently			Notes

Name: _____

Date: _____

Show What You Know!

___ / 4
Score

Notes _____

Name: _____

I Know Addition and Subtraction!

Addition

Date _____

Score [/]

Date _____

Score [/]

Date _____

Score [/]

Date _____

Score [/]

Subtraction

Date _____

Score [/]

Date _____

Score [/]

Date _____

Score [/]

Date _____

Score [/]

Fact Fluency

Fact Fluency for ___Addition___			
Student Name	Date	Score	Notes
Tasha	9/8	8/10	Knows facts fluently through 5, trouble with 8s, 9s, 10s
		/	
		/	
		/	
		/	
		/	
		/	
		/	
		/	
		/	
		/	
		/	
		/	

This page shows your class's fluency scores at a glance. It can be used for both addition and subtraction. Complete the title with *Addition* or *Subtraction*. Record student names in the left-hand column. Each column to the right allows you to record the date and the score for each fluency assessment. Use the *Notes* section to record observations and the strategies each student used.

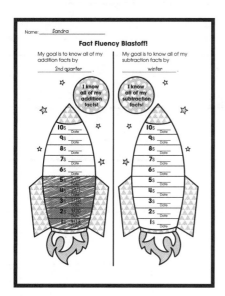

Use this page as a fun way for students to track their fact fluency progress. First, each student should set his addition and subtraction fact fluency goals. As students master their addition and subtraction facts, have them date and color the appropriate portion of each rocket. The student should color each moon when they have mastered all of their addition and subtraction facts.

Name: _Quan_	Week of: _4/15_		
Fact Fluency: Practice Makes Perfect!			
Day	Fact(s) I practiced	How I feel about these facts	Adult Signature
Monday	adding and subtracting 6s	☺ 😐 ☹	*Rw*
Tuesday		☺ 😐 ☹	
Wednesday		☺ 😐 ☹	
Thursday		☺ 😐 ☹	

I need more practice with ___adding 4s___

This page is a great way to get family members involved in helping their child learn his addition and subtraction facts. Each night of the week, students should record which fluency facts they practiced and how they felt about their progress. The parent, family member, or guardian should then sign the form. At the end of the week, the student should fill in which fluency facts he still needs help with.

Fact Fluency for _____

Student Name	Date	Score	Notes
		/	
		/	
		/	
		/	
		/	
		/	
		/	
		/	
		/	
		/	
		/	
		/	
		/	
		/	

Name: _____

Fact Fluency Blast Off!

My goal is to know all of my addition facts by

_____.

My goal is to know all of my subtraction facts by

_____.

I know all of my addition facts!

I know all of my subtraction facts!

10s _____
Date

9s _____
Date

8s _____
Date

7s _____
Date

6s _____
Date

5s _____
Date

4s _____
Date

3s _____
Date

2s _____
Date

1s _____
Date

10s _____
Date

9s _____
Date

8s _____
Date

7s _____
Date

6s _____
Date

5s _____
Date

4s _____
Date

3s _____
Date

2s _____
Date

1s _____
Date

Name: _____

Week of: _____

Fact Fluency: Practice Makes Perfect!

Day	Fact(s) I practiced	How I feel about these facts	Adult Signature
Monday		🙁 😐 🙂	
Tuesday		🙁 😐 🙂	
Wednesday		🙁 😐 🙂	
Thursday		🙁 😐 🙂	

I need more practice with _____

Number Sentences

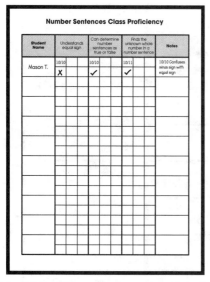

This page is ideal for keeping a record of your entire class's proficiency with number sentence concepts. Record student names in the left-hand column. As you present the skills, record the date and use a check mark system to indicate students' progress of each skill. With all of your students' progress at a glance, you can plan lessons and assign group work efficiently.

This assessment page can be used as a pretest and posttest evaluation on how well a student understands the concept of true number sentences. In a whole-group, small-group, or one-on-one setting, present a student with three true or false number sentences. The student should circle *True* or *Not True* and explain her reasoning in the right-hand column. Allow the student to record her overall score, color the thumbs-up or thumbs-down, and record her thoughts about what she can do next time to help her solve word problems.

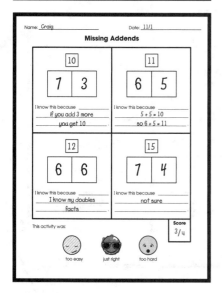

This assessment page can be used as a pretest and posttest evaluation on how well a student understands the concept of missing addends. In a whole-group, small-group, or one-on-one setting, present a student with four missing addend problems. For each problem, write the sum and one missing addend. The student should solve each problem, explain his reasoning, and record it in the space provided. Allow the student to record his overall score and color the appropriate face to show how he felt about the assignment.

Number Sentences Class Proficiency

Student Name	Understands equal sign			Can determine number sentences as true or false			Finds the unknown whole number in a number sentence			Notes

Name: _____   Date: _____

True Number Sentences

True Not True	How do I know?
	_____ _____ _____ _____
True Not True	How do I know?
	_____ _____ _____ _____ _____
True Not True	How do I know?
	_____ _____ _____ _____ _____

How did I do?

 /3
Score

Next time I will

_____
_____

Missing Addends

I know this because _____

_____

_____ .

I know this because _____

_____

_____ .

I know this because _____

_____

_____ .

I know this because _____

_____

_____ .

Score

/ 4

This activity was:

too easy   just right   too hard

Number and Operations in Base Ten
Standards Crosswalk

Kindergarten
Counting and Cardinality
Know number names and the count sequence.
• Count to 100 by ones and tens.
• Count forward from a given number.
• Write and represent numbers from 0 to 20.
Count to tell the number of objects.
• Understand the relationship between numbers and quantities.
• Count to answer "How many?" questions with up to 20 objects in a formation or up to 10 scattered objects.
• Count out a given number of objects from 1 to 20.
Compare numbers.
• Compare two groups of objects and identify them as greater than, less than, or equal to one another.
• Compare two written numerals between 1 and 10.
Work with numbers 11–19 to gain foundations for place value.
• Compose and decompose numbers from 11 to 19 into tens and ones and record with drawings or equations.

Second Grade
Understand place value.
• Understand that the digits of a three-digit number represent amounts of hundreds, tens, and ones.
• 100 can be thought of as a bundle of 10 tens, or a "hundred."
• The multiples of 100 (through 900) refer to 1–9 hundreds, 0 tens, and 0 ones.
• Count within 1,000.
• Skip-count by 5s, 10s, and 100s.
• Read and write numbers to 1,000 using numerals, number names, and expanded form.
• Use >, =, and < to compare two three-digit numbers.
Use place value understanding and properties of operations to add and subtract.
• Fluently add and subtract within 100.
• Add up to four two-digit numbers.
• Add and subtract within 1,000, relating the strategies used to a written method.
• Mentally add or subtract 10 or 100 to or from a given number 100–900.
• Explain why addition and subtraction strategies work.

Number and Operations in Base Ten
Concepts Checklist

Concept		Dates Taught			

Counting to 120

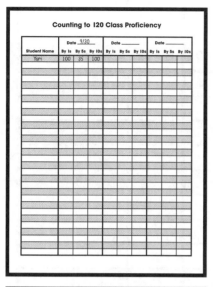

Use this page to individually assess each student's ability to rote count to 120 by 1s, 5s, and 10s. Each quarter (or another specified time frame of your choice), listen to the student count up to 120 by 1s. Record the last number the student counted up to in the *By 1s* column. Then, repeat the process to assess the student's ability to count to 120 by 5s and 10s.

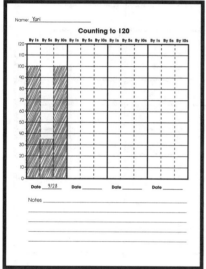

Use this page at home or in the classroom to allow each student to keep track of her progress in counting to 120. After each assessment, have the student to color in the chart to record her progress in counting to 120 by 1s, 5s, and 10s. Use the *Notes* section to record helpful information, such as specific numbers the student struggled with. Use this page as a portfolio tool for conferences with parents or students.

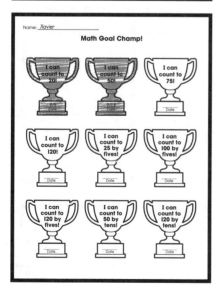

This page is a fun way for students to keep track of their ability to count to 120. Each time a student masters one of the goals listed in a trophy, allow him to write the date and color the corresponding trophy. Insert this page in a student's math portfolio to show progression of counting skills over time.

Counting to 120 Class Proficiency

Student Name	Date _____			Date _____			Date _____		
	By 1s	By 5s	By 10s	By 1s	By 5s	By 10s	By 1s	By 5s	By 10s

Name: _____

Counting to 120

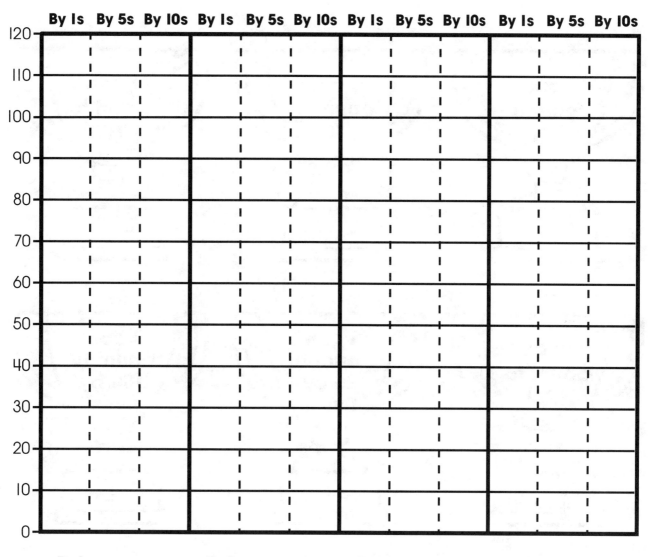

| | By 1s | By 5s | By 10s | By 1s | By 5s | By 10s | By 1s | By 5s | By 10s | By 1s | By 5s | By 10s |

Date _____   Date _____   Date _____   Date _____

Notes _____

_____

_____

_____

_____

Name: _____

Math Goal Champ!

I can count to 20!
Date _____

I can count to 50!
Date _____

I can count to 75!
Date _____

I can count to 120!
Date _____

I can count to 25 by fives!
Date _____

I can count to 100 by fives!
Date _____

I can count to 120 by fives!
Date _____

I can count to 50 by tens!
Date _____

I can count to 120 by tens!
Date _____

Reading and Writing Numbers to 120

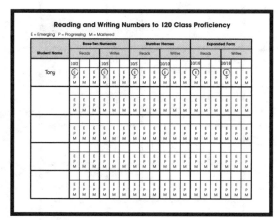

This page is ideal for keeping a record of your entire class's proficiency with reading and writing numbers to 120. Record student names in the left-hand column. As you assess the skills, record the date and circle *E*, *P*, or *M* (see the rating scale at the top of the page) to indicate the student's progress with each skill. This page allows you to see at a glance which students have mastered each skill and which students need more help.

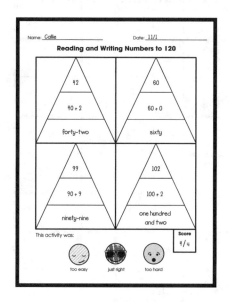

This page can be used for one-on-one assessments or in a guided math group. Starting at the top of the pyramid, students should fill in a number that you have said aloud. Then, each student should write the number's expanded form and the number name in the other pyramid sections. Allow students to record their overall score and color a face to rate how they felt about the assignment.

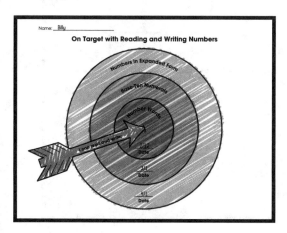

Students can take ownership and celebrate their learning with this page. Once a student can read and write number words, base ten numerals, and numbers in expanded form to 120, he should color the ring of the corresponding target. Have students record the date of mastery for each skill as well. Once all the sections have been colored, he can color the arrow to celebrate that he knows how to read and write numbers to 120.

Reading and Writing Numbers to 120 Class Proficiency

E = Emerging   P = Progressing   M = Mastered

Student Name	Base-Ten Numerals		Number Names		Expanded Form	
	Reads	Writes	Reads	Writes	Reads	Writes
	E P M	E P M	E P M	E P M	E P M	E P M
	E P M	E P M	E P M	E P M	E P M	E P M
	E P M	E P M	E P M	E P M	E P M	E P M
	E P M	E P M	E P M	E P M	E P M	E P M
	E P M	E P M	E P M	E P M	E P M	E P M

Name: _____ Date: _____

Reading and Writing Numbers to 120

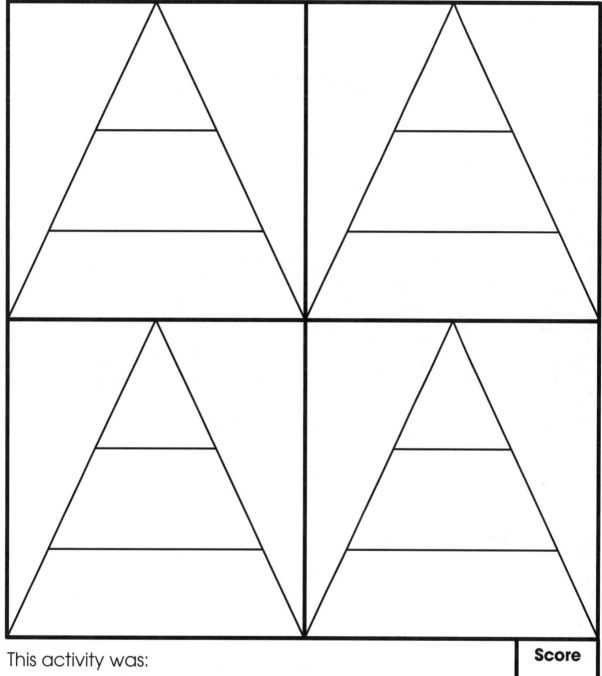

This activity was:

too easy

just right

too hard

Score

/4

Name: _____

On Target with Reading and Writing Numbers

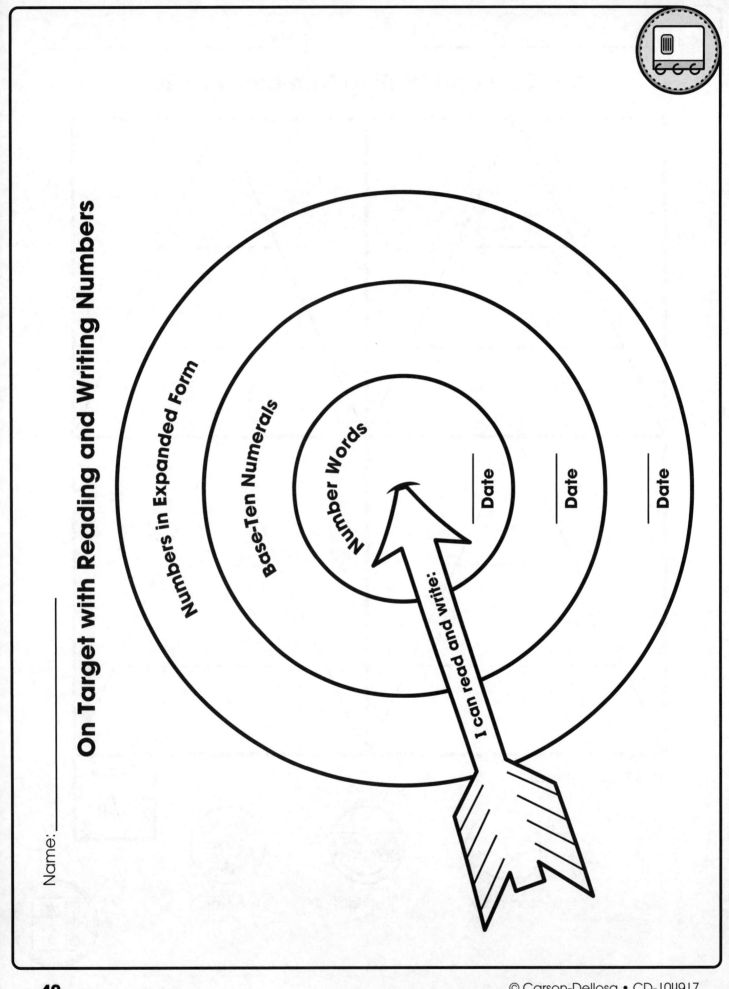

Numbers in Expanded Form

Base-Ten Numerals

Number Words

I can read and write:

_____
Date

_____
Date

_____
Date

Place Value

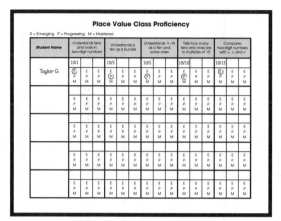

This page is ideal for keeping a record of your entire class's proficiency in understanding place value. Record student names in the left-hand column. As you assess the skills, record the date and circle *E*, *P*, or *M* (see the rating scale at the top of the page) to show the progress of each skill. This sheet can be also be used to present place value data at principal-teacher or grade-level meetings.

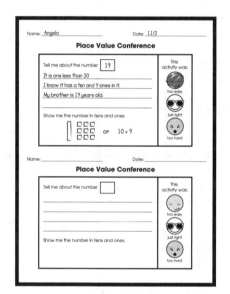

This conferencing page can be used to note a student's level of progress in understanding place value. It can also be used as proof of mastery to insert into a student's math portfolio. In a one-on-one conference with a student, assign a number for her to tell you about. Record her answers. Then, have her show you the number in tens and ones. At the end of the assessment, have her color a face to show how she felt about the activity.

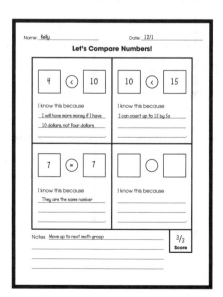

Once students have a working knowledge of place value, use this page to assess their knowledge of comparing one- and two-digit numbers. You or the student should fill in the two squares with two numbers. The student should fill in the circle with a comparison symbol. Students should give reasons for their answers in the spaces provided. Record the number correct over the total problems given in the *Score* box, and use the *Notes* section to record any strengths, weaknesses, or observations.

Place Value Class Proficiency

E = Emerging   P = Progressing   M = Mastered

Student Name	Understands tens and ones in two-digit numbers			Understands a ten as a bundle			Understands 11–19 as a ten and some ones			Tells how many tens and ones are in multiples of 10			Compares two-digit numbers with >, <, and =		
	E P M	E P M	E P M	E P M	E P M	E P M	E P M	E P M	E P M	E P M	E P M	E P M	E P M	E P M	E P M
	E P M	E P M	E P M	E P M	E P M	E P M	E P M	E P M	E P M	E P M	E P M	E P M	E P M	E P M	E P M
	E P M	E P M	E P M	E P M	E P M	E P M	E P M	E P M	E P M	E P M	E P M	E P M	E P M	E P M	E P M
	E P M	E P M	E P M	E P M	E P M	E P M	E P M	E P M	E P M	E P M	E P M	E P M	E P M	E P M	E P M
	E P M	E P M	E P M	E P M	E P M	E P M	E P M	E P M	E P M	E P M	E P M	E P M	E P M	E P M	E P M

Name: _____   Date: _____

Place Value Conference

Tell me about the number [ ] .

_____

_____

_____

_____

Show me the number in tens and ones.

This activity was:

too easy

just right

too hard

Name: _____   Date: _____

Place Value Conference

Tell me about the number [ ] .

_____

_____

_____

_____

Show me the number in tens and ones.

This activity was:

too easy

just right

too hard

Name: _____   Date: _____

Let's Compare Numbers!

☐ ◯ ☐

I know this because

_____

_____

_____ .

☐ ◯ ☐

I know this because

_____

_____

_____ .

☐ ◯ ☐

I know this because

_____

_____

_____ .

☐ ◯ ☐

I know this because

_____

_____

_____ .

Notes _____

_____

_____

/

Score

Addition and Subtraction within 100

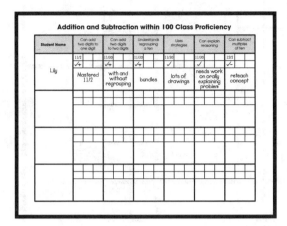

This page is ideal for keeping a record of your entire class's proficiency in understanding place value. Record student names in the left-hand column. As you assess the skills, record the date and a rating scale of your choosing (such as a check mark system) to indicate the progress of each skill. Use the blank space in each column to record strengths, weaknesses, and areas to focus on. This sheet can be also be useful at principal-teacher or grade-level meetings.

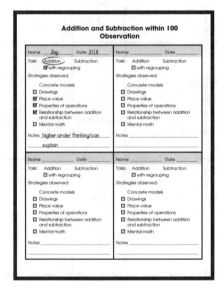

Use this page to observe a student during a math assignment. Record the student's name, the date, the task assigned, and any addition or subtraction strategies you observe the student using. Use the *Notes* section to record strengths and areas to focus on, as well as specific observations. If desired, print this page on adhesive label sheets to keep on a clipboard (visit our website for a free downloadable template). This makes conferencing and moving logs to student folders quick and easy.

Use this fun page to allow students to take ownership and celebrate their learning of addition and subtraction within 100. Students should date and color the corresponding parts of the ice-cream sundae as they master each skill. When a student can teach the skill to someone else, then ask the student to color the cherry on top of the skill.

Addition and Subtraction within 100 Class Proficiency

Student Name	Can add two digits to one digit	Can add two digits to two digits	Understands regrouping a ten	Uses strategies	Can explain reasoning	Can subtract multiples of ten

Addition and Subtraction within 100
Observation

Name _____ Date _____

Task: Addition   Subtraction
    ☐ with regrouping

Strategies observed:

    Concrete models
☐ Drawings
☐ Place value
☐ Properties of operations
☐ Relationship between addition
    and subtraction
☐ Mental math

Notes _____

_____

Name _____ Date _____

Task: Addition   Subtraction
    ☐ with regrouping

Strategies observed:

    Concrete models
☐ Drawings
☐ Place value
☐ Properties of operations
☐ Relationship between addition
    and subtraction
☐ Mental math

Notes _____

_____

Name _____ Date _____

Task: Addition   Subtraction
    ☐ with regrouping

Strategies observed:

    Concrete models
☐ Drawings
☐ Place value
☐ Properties of operations
☐ Relationship between addition
    and subtraction
☐ Mental math

Notes _____

_____

Name _____ Date _____

Task: Addition   Subtraction
    ☐ with regrouping

Strategies observed:

    Concrete models
☐ Drawings
☐ Place value
☐ Properties of operations
☐ Relationship between addition
    and subtraction
☐ Mental math

Notes _____

_____

Name: _____

I Can Add and Subtract!

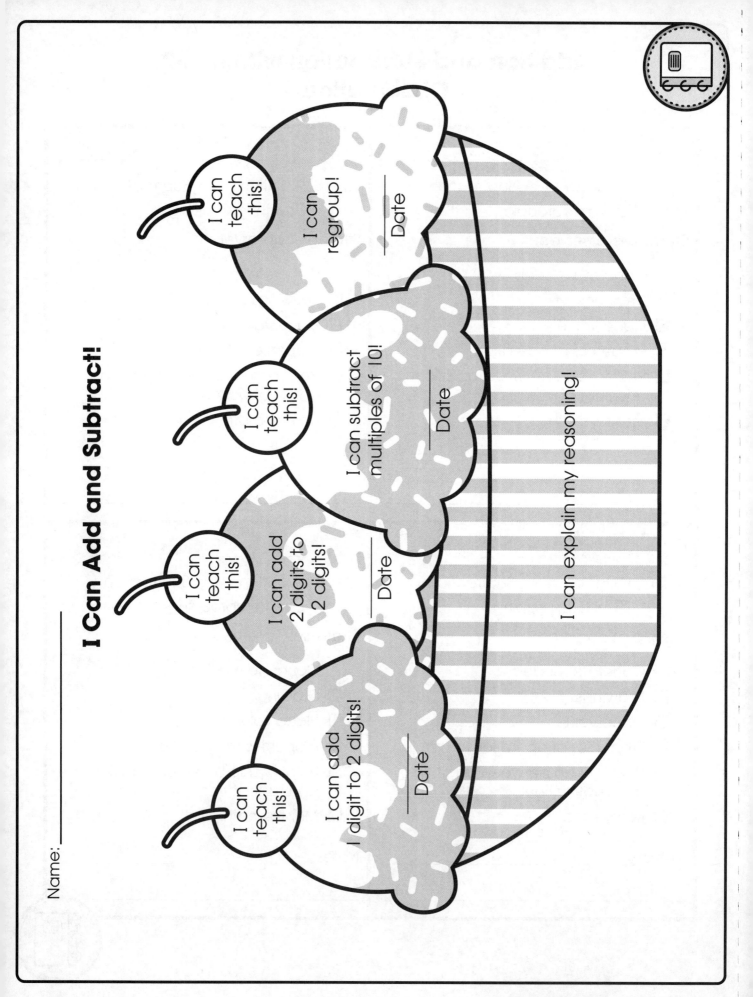

I can teach this!

I can regroup!

_____
Date

I can teach this!

I can subtract multiples of 10!

_____
Date

I can teach this!

I can add 2 digits to 2 digits!

_____
Date

I can teach this!

I can add 1 digit to 2 digits!

_____
Date

I can explain my reasoning!

Measurement and Data
Standards Crosswalk

Kindergarten

Describe and compare measurable attributes.
- Understand what can be measured.
- Compare two objects using a measurable attribute to determine which has more of or less of the attribute.

Classify objects and count the number of objects in each category.
- Classify and sort objects into categories.
- Count the total in each category and sort by count.

Second Grade

Measure and estimate lengths in standard units.
- Measure the length of an object by selecting and using appropriate tools.
- Measure the length of an object using two different length units and relate the measurements to the units used.
- Estimate lengths using units of inches, feet, centimeters, and meters.
- Measure to determine how much longer one object is than another.

Relate addition and subtraction to length.
- Use addition and subtraction within 100 to solve word problems involving lengths given in the same units.
- Represent whole numbers as lengths from 0 on a number line and represent whole-number sums and differences within 100 on a number line.

Work with time and money.
- Tell and write time from analog and digital clocks to the nearest five minutes, using *am* and *pm*.
- Solve word problems involving dollar bills, quarters, dimes, nickels, and pennies, using the $ and ¢ symbols appropriately.

Represent and interpret data.
- Measure objects and represent measurements on a line plot (to the nearest whole unit).
- Draw a picture graph and a bar graph (with single-unit scales) to represent up to four categories.
- Solve simple addition, subtraction, and comparison problems using information given in a graph.

Measurement and Data Concepts Checklist

Concept		Dates Taught				

Measuring Length and Time

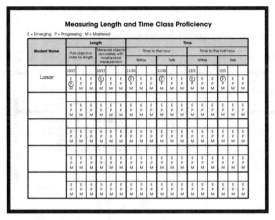

This page is ideal for keeping a record of your entire class's proficiency in length and time measurement skills. Record student names in the left-hand column. As you present the skills, record the date and circle *E*, *P*, or *M* (see the rating scale at the top of the page) to indicate students' progress of each skill. This sheet can also be used to present measurement skills data at principal-teacher or grade-level meetings.

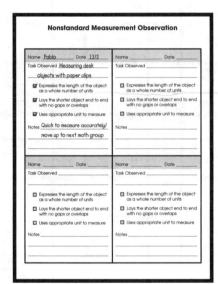

Use this page to observe a student during a measurement skills task. Record the student's name, the date, and the task assigned. Check the boxes as they apply. Use the *Notes* section to record strengths and areas to focus on, as well as specific observations. If desired, print this page on adhesive label sheets to keep on a clipboard (visit our website for a free downloadable template). This makes conferencing and moving logs to student folders quick and easy.

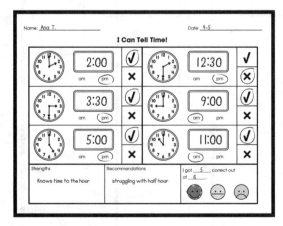

Use this page to assess a student's level of understanding of telling time to the hour and to the half-hour. For each space, say a time and have her complete the analog and digital clocks to match. Describe a real-life scenario and have her circle *am* or *pm*. Circle the check mark or the *X* to score the work. Have her record her overall score and color a face to show how she felt about the activity. Record strengths and recommendations at the bottom of the page.

Measuring Length and Time Class Proficiency

E = Emerging   P = Progressing   M = Mastered

Student Name	Length		Time			
	Puts objects in order by length	Measures objects accurately with nonstandard measurement	Time to the hour		Time to the half-hour	
			Writes	Tells	Writes	Tells
	E P M	E P M	E P M	E P M	E P M	E P M
	E P M	E P M	E P M	E P M	E P M	E P M
	E P M	E P M	E P M	E P M	E P M	E P M
	E P M	E P M	E P M	E P M	E P M	E P M
	E P M	E P M	E P M	E P M	E P M	E P M
	E P M	E P M	E P M	E P M	E P M	E P M
	E P M	E P M	E P M	E P M	E P M	E P M
	E P M	E P M	E P M	E P M	E P M	E P M
	E P M	E P M	E P M	E P M	E P M	E P M
	E P M	E P M	E P M	E P M	E P M	E P M
	E P M	E P M	E P M	E P M	E P M	E P M
	E P M	E P M	E P M	E P M	E P M	E P M
	E P M	E P M	E P M	E P M	E P M	E P M
	E P M	E P M	E P M	E P M	E P M	E P M
	E P M	E P M	E P M	E P M	E P M	E P M

Nonstandard Measurement Observation

Name _____ Date _____

Task Observed _____

_____

- ☐ Expresses the length of the object as a whole number of units
- ☐ Lays the shorter object end to end with no gaps or overlaps
- ☐ Uses appropriate unit to measure

Notes _____

_____

_____

Name _____ Date _____

Task Observed _____

_____

- ☐ Expresses the length of the object as a whole number of units
- ☐ Lays the shorter object end to end with no gaps or overlaps
- ☐ Uses appropriate unit to measure

Notes _____

_____

_____

Name _____ Date _____

Task Observed _____

_____

- ☐ Expresses the length of the object as a whole number of units
- ☐ Lays the shorter object end to end with no gaps or overlaps
- ☐ Uses appropriate unit to measure

Notes _____

_____

_____

Name _____ Date _____

Task Observed _____

_____

- ☐ Expresses the length of the object as a whole number of units
- ☐ Lays the shorter object end to end with no gaps or overlaps
- ☐ Uses appropriate unit to measure

Notes _____

_____

_____

I Can Tell Time!

Name: _____

Date: _____

	✓	✗		✓	✗		✓	✗

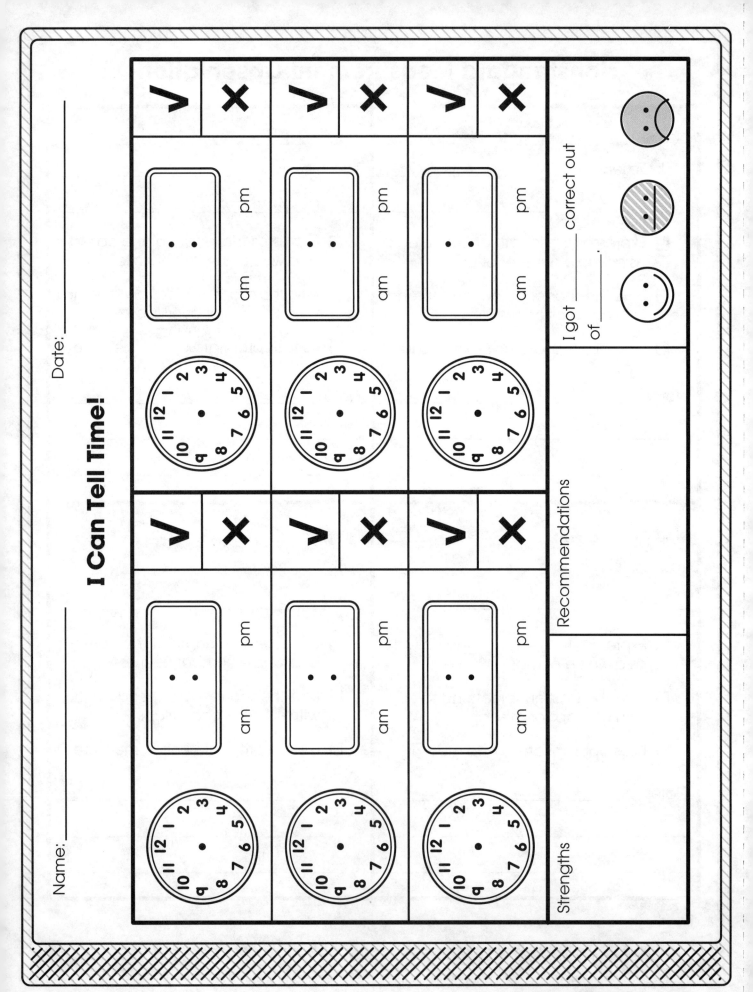

Strengths

Recommendations

I got _____ correct out of _____.

Graphs and Data

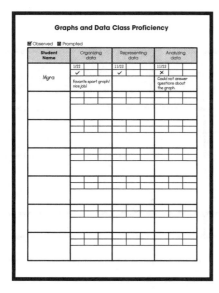

Student mastery of graphing and data skills can be seen at a glance on this easy-to-use page. Write student names in the left-hand column. Use the scoring guide at the top of the page to mark each student's level of mastery with each skill as a unit progresses. Use the blank space in each column to record scores, observations, or notes.

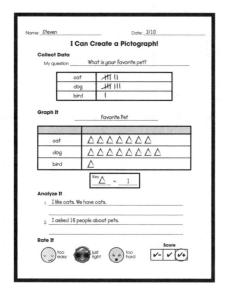

Allow students to show what they know about making pictographs in this student assessment activity. Each student should consider what data he wants to gather, either at home or at school (the title should reflect this). He should use tally marks to record his data in the top chart. Then, have him graph the collected data on the blank pictograph. He should analyze the graph by writing two observations or questions about the information in the graph. Finally, he should color a face to reflect how he felt about the activity. Score the student's work by circling the correct check mark.

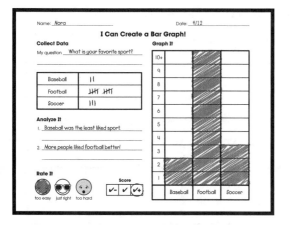

Use this page as proof of students' mastery in constructing bar graphs. Have each student collect data on a question of her choosing. She should write her question and use tally marks to record the data in the chart on the left. Then, have her graph the data on the blank bar graph. She should analyze the graph by writing two observations or questions about information in the graph. Finally, she should color a face to reflect how she felt about the activity. Score the student's work by circling the correct check mark.

Graphs and Data Class Proficiency

☑ Observed ☒ Prompted

Student Name	Organizing data			Representing data			Analyzing data		

56

I Can Create a Pictograph!

Collect Data

My question _____

Graph It

_____

Key
_____ = _____

Analyze It

1. _____

   _____

2. _____

   _____

Rate It

too easy   just right   too hard

Score		
✔−	✔	✔+

Name: _____

Date: _____

I Can Create a Bar Graph!

Collect Data

My question _____

_____

Graph It

10+			
9			
8			
7			
6			
5			
4			
3			
2			
1			

Analyze It

1. _____

_____

2. _____

Rate It

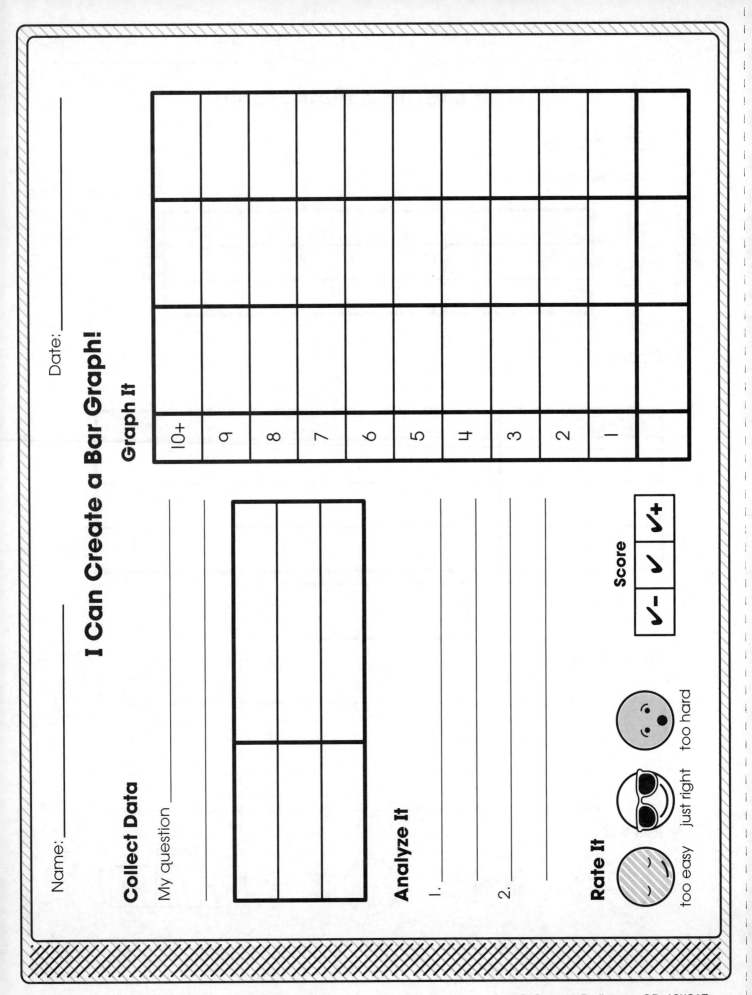

too easy   just right   too hard

Score

| ✔− | ✔ | ✔+ |

Geometry
Standards Crosswalk

Kindergarten

Identify and describe shapes (squares, circles, triangles, rectangles, hexagons, cubes, cones, cylinders, and spheres).

- Describe, name, and identify objects in the environment using shape names.
- Describe the relative positions of objects.
- Correctly name shapes regardless of size or orientation.
- Identify plane (2-D) and solid shapes (3-D).

Analyze, compare, create, and compose shapes.

- Describe, analyze, and compare two- and three-dimensional shapes and their attributes.
- Model real-world shapes by building and drawing them.
- Combine simple shapes to form larger shapes.

Second Grade

Reason with shapes and their attributes.

- Recognize and draw shapes with specific attributes.
- Identify triangles, quadrilaterals, pentagons, hexagons, and cubes.
- Partition a rectangle into rows and columns of same-size squares and count to find the total number of them.
- Partition circles and rectangles into two, three, or four equal shares, using the words *halves, thirds, half of, a fourth of,* etc., to describe them.
- Describe a divided whole as two halves, three thirds, four fourths.
- Recognize that equal shares of identical wholes may not have the same shape.

Geometry Concepts Checklist

Concept		Dates Taught				

Shapes

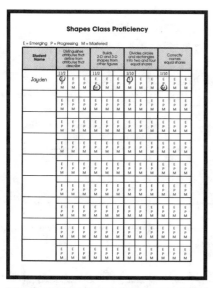

This page is perfect for tracking proficiency in geometry skills. Record student names in the left-hand column. As you assess the skills, record the date and circle *E, P,* or *M* (see the rating scale at the top of the page) to indicate the progress of each skill. This will allow you to see at a glance which students have mastered each skill and which students need more help.

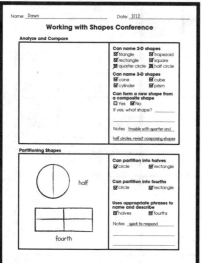

For a conference on identifying and composing shapes, present the student with a pattern block shape (or picture of a shape) of your choosing. Check any boxes that apply to the student's responses. Then, repeat the process with a solid shape (or picture of a solid shape). Use the *Notes* section to record any strengths, weaknesses, or observations. For a conference on partitioning shapes, present the student with a circle or rectangle and ask her to divide it into halves and/or fourths. Check any boxes that apply. Use the *Notes* section to record any strengths, weaknesses, or observations.

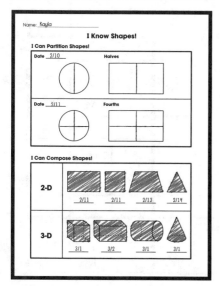

This sheet is perfect for students to track their mastery of composing and partitioning shapes. As students master partitioning shapes, allow each student to partition the shape and record the date. For composing shapes, allow the student to record the date and color each shape that she is able to compose from other shapes. This page can be inserted into a student's math portfolio to show proof of mastery.

Shapes Class Proficiency

E = Emerging   P = Progressing   M = Mastered

Student Name	Distinguishes attributes that define from attributes that describe			Builds 2-D and 3-D shapes from other figures			Divides circles and rectangles into two and four equal shares			Correctly names equal shares		
	E P M	E P M	E P M	E P M	E P M	E P M	E P M	E P M	E P M	E P M	E P M	E P M
	E P M	E P M	E P M	E P M	E P M	E P M	E P M	E P M	E P M	E P M	E P M	E P M
	E P M	E P M	E P M	E P M	E P M	E P M	E P M	E P M	E P M	E P M	E P M	E P M
	E P M	E P M	E P M	E P M	E P M	E P M	E P M	E P M	E P M	E P M	E P M	E P M
	E P M	E P M	E P M	E P M	E P M	E P M	E P M	E P M	E P M	E P M	E P M	E P M
	E P M	E P M	E P M	E P M	E P M	E P M	E P M	E P M	E P M	E P M	E P M	E P M
	E P M	E P M	E P M	E P M	E P M	E P M	E P M	E P M	E P M	E P M	E P M	E P M
	E P M	E P M	E P M	E P M	E P M	E P M	E P M	E P M	E P M	E P M	E P M	E P M
	E P M	E P M	E P M	E P M	E P M	E P M	E P M	E P M	E P M	E P M	E P M	E P M

Name: _____   Date: _____

Working with Shapes Conference

Analyze and Compare

<table>
<tr>
<td>

</td>
<td>

Can name 2-D shapes

☐ triangle   ☐ trapezoid

☐ rectangle   ☐ square

☐ quarter circle   ☐ half circle

Can name 3-D shapes

☐ cone   ☐ cube

☐ cylinder   ☐ prism

Can form a new shape from a composite shape

☐ Yes   ☐ No

If yes, what shape? _____

_____

Notes _____

_____

</td>
</tr>
</table>

Partitioning Shapes

<table>
<tr>
<td>

</td>
<td>

Can partition into halves

☐ circle   ☐ rectangle

Can partition into fourths

☐ circle   ☐ rectangle

Uses appropriate phrases to name and describe

☐ halves   ☐ fourths

Notes _____

_____

_____

</td>
</tr>
</table>

Name: _____

I Know Shapes!

I Can Partition Shapes!

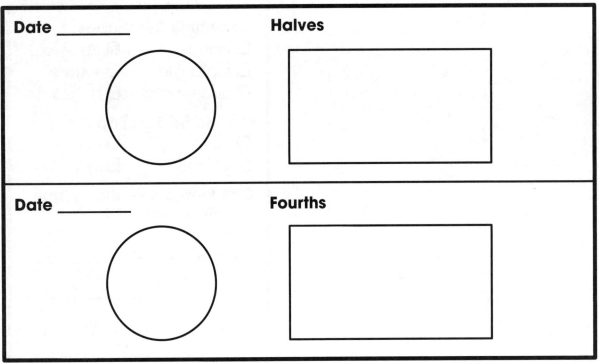

Date _____   **Halves**

Date _____   **Fourths**

I Can Compose Shapes!

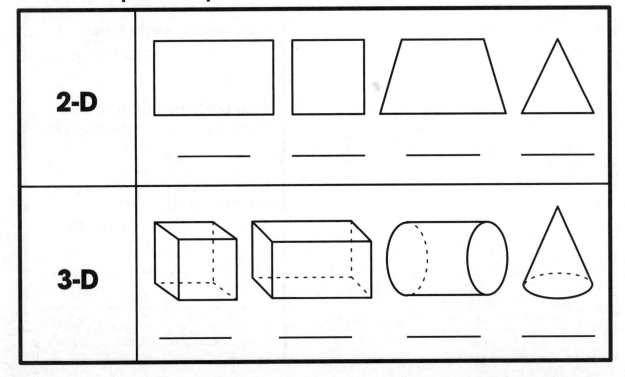

2-D

3-D

Reading: Literature
Standards Crosswalk

Kindergarten

Key Ideas and Details

With prompting and support:
- Ask and answer questions about key details in a text.
- Retell familiar stories, including key details.
- Identify characters, settings, and major events in a story.

Craft and Structure
- Ask and answer questions about unknown words in a text.
- Recognize common types of texts.
- With prompting and support, name the author and illustrator of a story and define their roles in telling the story.

Integration of Knowledge and Ideas

With prompting and support:
- Describe the relationship between illustrations and the story.
- Compare and contrast the experiences of characters in familiar stories.

Range of Reading and Level of Text Complexity
- Participate in group reading activities with purpose and understanding.

Second Grade

Key Ideas and Details
- Ask and answer such questions as *who, what, when, where, why,* and *how* about key details in a text.
- Recount stories, including fables and folktales from diverse cultures, and determine their central messages, lessons, or morals.
- Describe how characters in a story respond to major events and challenges.

Craft and Structure
- Describe how words and phrases supply rhythm and meaning in a story, poem, or song.
- Describe the overall structure of a story.
- Understand the purpose of a story's beginning and ending.
- Acknowledge differences in the points of view of characters.
- Use different voices for each character when reading dialogue aloud.

Integration of Knowledge and Ideas
- Use information from illustrations and words in text to demonstrate understanding of its characters, setting, or plot.
- Compare and contrast two or more versions of the same story by different authors or from different cultures.

Range of Reading and Level of Text Complexity
- By the end of the year, proficiently read and comprehend literature in the grades 2–3 text complexity band.

Reading: Literature Concepts Checklist

Concept		Dates Taught				

Literature Comprehension

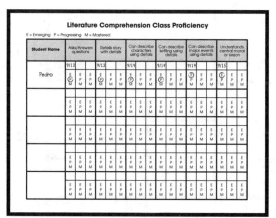

Use this page to track your class's proficiency levels in literature comprehension. Record student names in the left-hand column. As you assess the skills, record the date and circle *E*, *P*, or *M* (see the rating scale at the top of the page) to indicate the progress with each skill. This will allow you to see at a glance which students have mastered each skill and which students need more help. Use this sheet as a reference tool for principal-teacher or grade-level meetings.

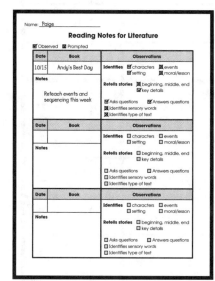

This page is ideal for a student assessment on a recently read book. Record the title of the book being assessed and the date. Then, use the observation checklist to check the concepts that were observed (note the scoring guide at the top of the page). Use the *Notes* section to record any notes, concerns, or concepts that need to be retaught. This page can be used three times to show progression of skills in reading comprehension throughout the year.

This page is ideal for sending home to parents so they can see their child's progress in retelling a story. Encourage family members to read a book to or with their child. Then, the student should fill out the book report with pictures or words. Finally, the student should color the thumbs-up or thumbs-down to rate how they felt about the book and write a sentence to explain why. In the *Notes* section, the family member should describe how the child read the book.

Literature Comprehension Class Proficiency

E = Emerging   P = Progressing   M = Mastered

Student Name	Asks/Answers questions			Retells story with details			Can describe characters using details			Can describe setting using details			Can describe major events using details			Understands central moral or lesson		
	E P M	E P M	E P M	E P M	E P M	E P M	E P M	E P M	E P M	E P M	E P M	E P M	E P M	E P M	E P M	E P M	E P M	E P M
	E P M	E P M	E P M	E P M	E P M	E P M	E P M	E P M	E P M	E P M	E P M	E P M	E P M	E P M	E P M	E P M	E P M	E P M
	E P M	E P M	E P M	E P M	E P M	E P M	E P M	E P M	E P M	E P M	E P M	E P M	E P M	E P M	E P M	E P M	E P M	E P M
	E P M	E P M	E P M	E P M	E P M	E P M	E P M	E P M	E P M	E P M	E P M	E P M	E P M	E P M	E P M	E P M	E P M	E P M
	E P M	E P M	E P M	E P M	E P M	E P M	E P M	E P M	E P M	E P M	E P M	E P M	E P M	E P M	E P M	E P M	E P M	E P M

Name: _____

Reading Notes for Literature

☑ Observed   ☒ Prompted

Date	Book	Observations
		Identifies ☐ characters ☐ events ☐ setting ☐ moral/lesson **Retells stories** ☐ beginning, middle, end ☐ key details ☐ Asks questions ☐ Answers questions ☐ Identifies sensory words ☐ Identifies type of text
Notes		
Date	Book	Observations
		Identifies ☐ characters ☐ events ☐ setting ☐ moral/lesson **Retells stories** ☐ beginning, middle, end ☐ key details ☐ Asks questions ☐ Answers questions ☐ Identifies sensory words ☐ Identifies type of text
Notes		
Date	Book	Observations
		Identifies ☐ characters ☐ events ☐ setting ☐ moral/lesson **Retells stories** ☐ beginning, middle, end ☐ key details ☐ Asks questions ☐ Answers questions ☐ Identifies sensory words ☐ Identifies type of text
Notes		

_____'s Book Report

I Love to Read!

_____
Title

_____
Author

_____
Illustrator

Character(s)	Setting
Beginning	Middle
End	**I give this book:** Why? _____ _____ _____

Parent/Teacher Notes _____

_____

_____

Tracking Reading

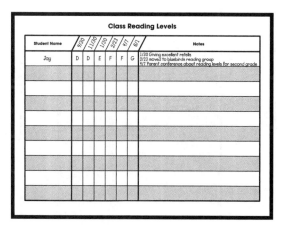

This page supplies class reading levels at a glance. Record student names in the left-hand column. Throughout the year, note the date and the student's current reading level with the scale you are accustomed to using. Use the *Notes* section to record strengths, weaknesses, or concerns. Additionally, this page is useful for assigning students to reading groups.

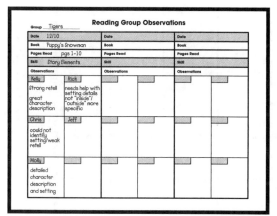

This page makes it easy to record reading group observations. Write the group name, date, book title, pages read, and the skill that is being observed. Then, as the reading group convenes, record notes on each reading group member.

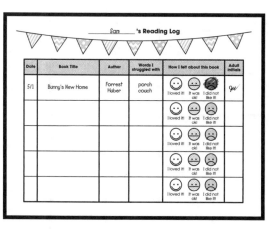

Have students use this reading log to keep track of their independent fiction reading or nonfiction reading. It can be used in the classroom or at home. The student, parent, or teacher should record the date, title, and author of the book. The student should write any words that they had trouble with while reading. Then, the student should color the appropriate face to show how they felt about the book. If using this page as an at-home log, have parents or guardians initial in the space provided.

Class Reading Levels

Student Name	Notes									

Reading Group Observations

Group _____

Date	Book	Pages Read	Skill	Observations			

_____'s Reading Log

Date	Book Title	Author	Words I struggled with	How I felt about this book	Adult initials
				☺ I loved it! ◐ It was ok! ☹ I did not like it!	
				☺ I loved it! ◐ It was ok! ☹ I did not like it!	
				☺ I loved it! ◐ It was ok! ☹ I did not like it!	
				☺ I loved it! ◐ It was ok! ☹ I did not like it!	
				☺ I loved it! ◐ It was ok! ☹ I did not like it!	

Reading: Informational Text
Standards Crosswalk

Kindergarten

Key Ideas and Details

With prompting and support:
- Ask and answer questions about key details in a text.
- Identify the main topic and retell key details of a text.
- Describe the connection between two individuals, events, ideas, or pieces of information in a text.

Craft and Structure
- Ask and answer questions about unknown words in a text.
- Identify the front cover, back cover, and title page of a book.
- Name the author and illustrator of a text and define their roles.

Integration of Knowledge and Ideas

With prompting and support:
- Describe the relationship between illustrations and the text.
- Identify the reasons an author gives to support points in a text.
- Identify basic similarities and differences between two texts on the same topic.

Range of Reading and Level of Text Complexity
- Participate in group reading activities with purpose and understanding.

Second Grade

Key Ideas and Details
- Ask and answer questions such as *who, what, when, where, why*, and *how* about key details in a text.
- Identify the main topic of a multi-paragraph text and the focus of specific paragraphs.
- Describe the connection between a series of historical events, scientific ideas or concepts, or steps in technical procedures in a text.

Craft and Structure
- Determine the meaning of words and phrases in a text.
- Use text features (captions, bold print, subheadings, glossaries, indexes, electronic menus, icons) to locate information.
- Identify the main purpose of a text, including the author's purpose.

Integration of Knowledge and Ideas
- Explain how specific images contribute to and clarify a text.
- Describe how reasons support specific points made in a text.
- Compare and contrast key points presented by two texts on the same topic.

Reading and Level of Text Complexity
- By the end of the year, read and comprehend informational texts in the grades 2–3 complexity band.

Reading: Informational Text
Concepts Checklist

Concept		Dates Taught				

Informational Text Comprehension

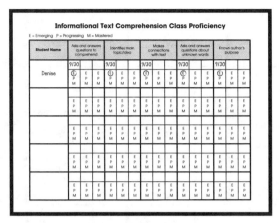

Use this page to track your class's proficiency levels with informational text comprehension. Record student names in the left-hand column. As the skills are assessed, record the date and circle *E, P,* or *M* (see the rating scale at the top of the page) to indicate the progress of each skill. This will allow you to see at a glance which students have mastered each skill and which students need more help. Use this sheet as a reference tool for principal-teacher or grade-level meetings.

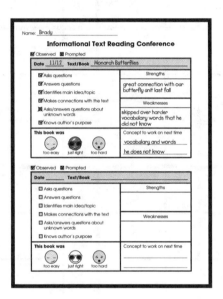

Use this page to conference one-on-one with a student about a recently read informational text, article, or book. Use the checklist on the left to review each element of reading comprehension with the student. Record strengths and weaknesses of the student's reading in the right column. Then, you and the student should decide on and record a concept to work on before the next conference. Finally, the student should color one of the corresponding faces to rate how she felt about the book.

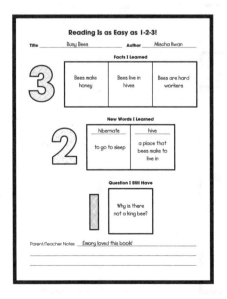

This page is ideal for sending home to parents so they can see their child's progress in reading and comprehending informational text. Encourage family members to read a nonfiction book to or with their student. Then, the student should fill out the graphic organizer with three new facts he learned, two new words that he learned and the definitions, and one question he still has about the text. At the bottom, the parent or teacher can use the *Notes* section to express any questions or concerns.

Informational Text Comprehension Class Proficiency

E = Emerging   P = Progressing   M = Mastered

Student Name	Asks and answers questions to comprehend			Identifies main topic/idea			Makes connections with text			Asks and answers questions about unknown words			Knows author's purpose		
	E P M	E P M	E P M	E P M	E P M	E P M	E P M	E P M	E P M	E P M	E P M	E P M	E P M	E P M	E P M
	E P M	E P M	E P M	E P M	E P M	E P M	E P M	E P M	E P M	E P M	E P M	E P M	E P M	E P M	E P M
	E P M	E P M	E P M	E P M	E P M	E P M	E P M	E P M	E P M	E P M	E P M	E P M	E P M	E P M	E P M
	E P M	E P M	E P M	E P M	E P M	E P M	E P M	E P M	E P M	E P M	E P M	E P M	E P M	E P M	E P M
	E P M	E P M	E P M	E P M	E P M	E P M	E P M	E P M	E P M	E P M	E P M	E P M	E P M	E P M	E P M

Name: _____

Informational Text Reading Conference

☑ Observed ☒ Prompted

Date _____ Text/Book _____	
☐ Asks questions	**Strengths**
☐ Answers questions	
☐ Identifies main idea/topic	
☐ Makes connections with the text	**Weaknesses**
☐ Asks/answers questions about unknown words	
☐ Knows author's purpose	

This book was

too easy   just right   too hard

Concept to work on next time

_____

_____

☑ Observed ☒ Prompted

Date _____ Text/Book _____	
☐ Asks questions	**Strengths**
☐ Answers questions	
☐ Identifies main idea/topic	
☐ Makes connections with the text	**Weaknesses**
☐ Asks/answers questions about unknown words	
☐ Knows author's purpose	

This book was

too easy   just right   too hard

Concept to work on next time

_____

_____

Reading Is as Easy as 1-2-3!

Title _____ **Author** _____

Facts I Learned

3

New Words I Learned

2

Question I Still Have

Parent/Teacher Notes _____

_____

_____

Informational Text Structure

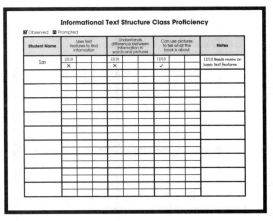

Use this page to track your class's proficiency levels with informational text structure. Record student names in the left-hand column. As you assess the skills, record the date and a score (see the scoring guide at the top of the page) to indicate the progress of each skill. This will allow you to see at a glance which students have mastered each skill and which students need more help.

Use this page to conference one-on-one with a student. For text structure, write the date and the title of the book you want to assess with the student. Write the text feature you would like the student to focus on and the page number where you can find it. Use the checklist to review each element of text structure with the student. For picture/illustrations, write the date and the title of the book you want to assess with the student. Write a short description of the picture or illustration you would like the student to focus on and the page number where you can find the item. Record any notes or concerns you have in the *Notes* sections.

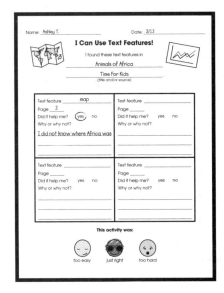

Use this page to allow students to take ownership of mastering the concept of informational text features. Have students choose a book that includes text features. Students should write the title and/or source of the text. As students read the book, they should take note of the various text features and how they aid in their understanding the text. Using this form, have students write the name and purpose of a text feature they found. Students should circle *yes* or *no* to tell if they thought the text feature was helpful and explain why it did or did not help. At the end of the activity, students should color a face to rate how they felt about the activity.

Informational Text Structure Class Proficiency

☑ Observed ☒ Prompted

Student Name	Uses text features to find information			Understands difference between information in words and pictures			Can use pictures to tell what the book is about			Notes

Text Structure: Text Features

☑ Observed   ☒ Prompted

Date _____

Text _____ pg. ___

Text Feature _____

- ☐ Student can name the text feature
- ☐ Student can tell where to find the text feature
- ☐ Student can tell how it is useful to the reader

Notes _____

_____

Date _____

Text _____ pg. ___

Text Feature _____

- ☐ Student can name the text feature
- ☐ Student can tell where to find the text feature
- ☐ Student can tell how it is useful to the reader

Notes _____

_____

Text Structure: Pictures/Illustrations

Date _____

Picture/Illustration _____

Text _____ pg. ___

- ☐ Student can tell the topic of the text by looking at the pictures or illustrations
- ☐ Student can find words in the text that tell about the pictures or illustrations
- ☐ Student can tell how the picture or illustration is useful

Notes _____

_____

Date _____

Picture/Illustration _____

Text _____ pg. ___

- ☐ Student can tell the topic of the text by looking at the pictures or illustrations
- ☐ Student can find words in the text that tell about the pictures or illustrations
- ☐ Student can tell how the picture or illustration is useful

Notes _____

_____

I Can Use Text Features!

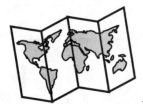

I found these text features in

_____

_____.

(title and/or source)

Text feature _____ Page _____ Did it help me? yes no Why or why not? _____ _____ _____	Text feature _____ Page _____ Did it help me? yes no Why or why not? _____ _____ _____
Text feature _____ Page _____ Did it help me? yes no Why or why not? _____ _____ _____	Text feature _____ Page _____ Did it help me? yes no Why or why not? _____ _____ _____

This activity was:

too easy   just right   too hard

Reading: Foundational Skills
Standards Crosswalk

Kindergarten

Print Concepts

- Follow words from left to right, top to bottom, and page by page.
- Recognize that spoken words are represented in written language by specific sequences of letters.
- Understand that words are separated by spaces in print.
- Recognize and name all upper- and lowercase letters of the alphabet.

Phonological Awareness

- Understand spoken words, syllables, and phonemes.
- Recognize and produce rhyming words.
- Count, pronounce, blend, and segment syllables in spoken words.
- Blend and segment onsets and rimes of single-syllable spoken words.
- Isolate and pronounce the initial, medial vowel, and final sounds in three-phoneme (CVC) words.
- Add or substitute individual sounds in one-syllable words to make new words.

Phonics and Word Recognition

- Know and apply grade-level phonics and word analysis skills in decoding words.
- Apply knowledge of one-to-one letter-sound correspondences by producing the primary sound or most frequent sounds for each consonant.
- Associate the long and short sounds with the common spellings for major vowels.
- Read common sight words.
- Distinguish between similarly spelled words by identifying the sounds that differ.

Fluency

- Read emergent-reader texts with purpose and understanding.

Second Grade

Print Concepts and Phonological Awareness end in first grade.

Phonics and Word Recognition

- Know and apply grade-level phonics and word analysis skills.
- Identify long and short vowels in regularly spelled one-syllable words.
- Know spelling-sound correspondences for additional common vowel teams.
- Decode regularly spelled two-syllable words with long vowels.
- Decode words with common prefixes and suffixes.
- Identify words with inconsistent but common spelling-sound correspondences.
- Recognize and read grade-appropriate, irregularly spelled words.

Fluency

- Read with sufficient accuracy and fluency to support comprehension.
- Read grade-level text with purpose and understanding.
- Read grade-level text orally with accuracy, appropriate rate, and expression on successive readings.
- Use context and rereading to confirm or self-correct word recognition and understanding.

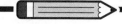

Reading: Foundational Skills
Concepts Checklist

Concept		Dates Taught				

Phonemic Awareness

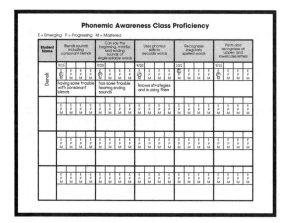

Use this page to keep track of your class's proficiency in phonemic awareness skills. Record student names in the left-hand column. As you present the skills, record the date and circle *E*, *P*, or *M* (see the rating scale at the top of the page) to indicate the progress of each skill. Use the blank area in each column to record any notes or concerns. Present this page at principal-teacher conferences or grade-level meetings to show progress of your students in the area of phonemic awareness skills.

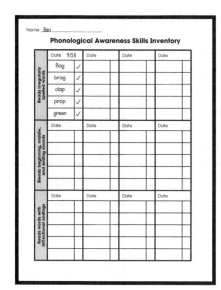

Use this skills inventory page for a more in-depth assessment of students' phonological awareness. Before each assessment, choose various words that correspond with each skill set on the page. Type or write them on index cards. Record the date of assessment and the words used for the assessment in the first column. As you present the student with the words, record how the student performed with each word in the appropriate space on the chart. Use this page to show progression of phonological skills at parent-teacher conferences.

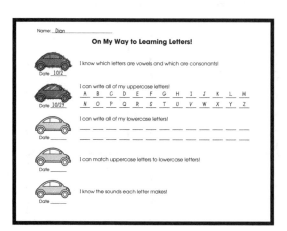

This page is useful for allowing students to track progress of their phonological awareness goals throughout the school year. As a student masters each skill, the student should write the date the goal was achieved and color the corresponding car. For the uppercase and lowercase letters, students should write each of the letters in a blank to prove mastery of the skill.

Phonemic Awareness Class Proficiency

E = Emerging   P = Progressing   M = Mastered

Student Name	Blends sounds including consonant blends				Can say the beginning, middle, and ending sounds of single-syllable words				Uses phonics skills to decode words				Recognizes irregularly spelled words				Prints and recognizes all upper- and lowercase letters			
	E P M	E P M	E P M	E P M	E P M	E P M	E P M	E P M	E P M	E P M	E P M	E P M	E P M	E P M	E P M	E P M	E P M	E P M	E P M	E P M
	E P M	E P M	E P M	E P M	E P M	E P M	E P M	E P M	E P M	E P M	E P M	E P M	E P M	E P M	E P M	E P M	E P M	E P M	E P M	E P M
	E P M	E P M	E P M	E P M	E P M	E P M	E P M	E P M	E P M	E P M	E P M	E P M	E P M	E P M	E P M	E P M	E P M	E P M	E P M	E P M
	E P M	E P M	E P M	E P M	E P M	E P M	E P M	E P M	E P M	E P M	E P M	E P M	E P M	E P M	E P M	E P M	E P M	E P M	E P M	E P M

Name: _____

Phonological Awareness Skills Inventory

Reads irregularly spelled words	Date		Date		Date		Date	

Blends beginning, middle, and ending sounds	Date		Date		Date		Date	

Reads words with inflectional endings	Date		Date		Date		Date	

On My Way to Learning Letters!

Name: _____

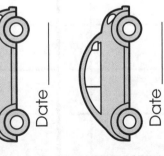

I know which letters are vowels and which are consonants!

I can write all of my uppercase letters!

I can write all of my lowercase letters!

I can match uppercase letters to lowercase letters!

I know the sounds each letter makes!

Date _____

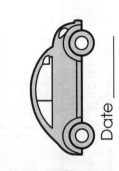

Vowel Sounds

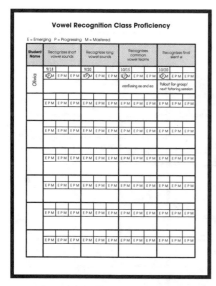

Use this page to keep a record of your class's proficiency in hearing and recognizing short and long vowel sounds, final *e*, and vowel teams in words. Record student names in the left-hand column. As you present the skills, record the date and circle *E*, *P*, or *M* (see the rating scale at the top of the page) to indicate the progress of each skill. Use the blank space at the bottom of each section to record any notes or concerns.

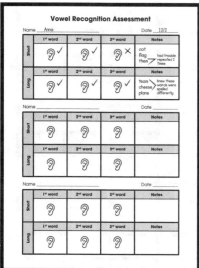

This page can be used to show student progress in recognizing vowel sounds. For each vowel sound, say three words to the student. If they can tell you they hear the vowel sound and can correctly identify it, place a check mark next to the ear. Place an *X* next to the ear if the student does not correctly identify the vowel sound in the word. Use the *Notes* sections to write the words presented or record any observations.

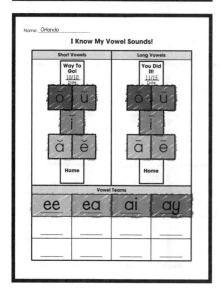

This page allows students to track their own progress in recognizing long and short vowel sounds and vowel teams. As the student masters each vowel sound, she should color the corresponding hopscotch block. When all of the vowel sounds have been mastered, the student should write the date on the top block of the hopscotch board. As a student masters various vowel team sounds, she should write the vowel team in a block at the bottom of the page and color it.

Vowel Recognition Class Proficiency

E = Emerging   P = Progressing   M = Mastered

Student Name	Recognizes short vowel sounds			Recognizes long vowel sounds			Recognizes common vowel teams			Recognizes final silent e		
	E P M	E P M	E P M	E P M	E P M	E P M	E P M	E P M	E P M	E P M	E P M	E P M
	E P M	E P M	E P M	E P M	E P M	E P M	E P M	E P M	E P M	E P M	E P M	E P M
	E P M	E P M	E P M	E P M	E P M	E P M	E P M	E P M	E P M	E P M	E P M	E P M
	E P M	E P M	E P M	E P M	E P M	E P M	E P M	E P M	E P M	E P M	E P M	E P M
	E P M	E P M	E P M	E P M	E P M	E P M	E P M	E P M	E P M	E P M	E P M	E P M
	E P M	E P M	E P M	E P M	E P M	E P M	E P M	E P M	E P M	E P M	E P M	E P M
	E P M	E P M	E P M	E P M	E P M	E P M	E P M	E P M	E P M	E P M	E P M	E P M

Vowel Recognition Assessment

Name _____ Date _____

	1st word	2nd word	3rd word	Notes
Short	👂	👂	👂	

	1st word	2nd word	3rd word	Notes
Long	👂	👂	👂	

Name _____ Date _____

	1st word	2nd word	3rd word	Notes
Short	👂	👂	👂	

	1st word	2nd word	3rd word	Notes
Long	👂	👂	👂	

Name _____ Date _____

	1st word	2nd word	3rd word	Notes
Short	👂	👂	👂	

	1st word	2nd word	3rd word	Notes
Long	👂	👂	👂	

Name: _____

I Know My Vowel Sounds!

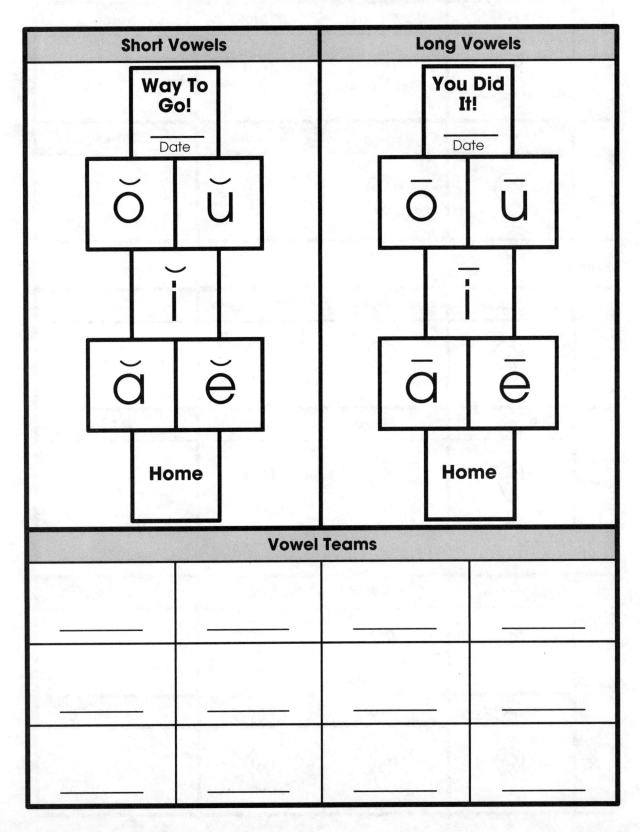

Short Vowels	Long Vowels

Short Vowels

Way To Go!
_____ Date

ŏ   ŭ

ĭ

ă   ĕ

Home

Long Vowels

You Did It!
_____ Date

ō   ū

ī

ā   ē

Home

Vowel Teams

_____	_____	_____	_____
_____	_____	_____	_____
_____	_____	_____	_____

Blends and Digraphs

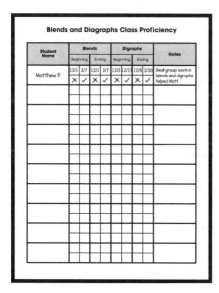

Use this page to keep a record of your class's proficiency with blends and digraphs. Record student names in the left-hand column. As you present the skills, record the date and score of the assessment (or use a rating system of your choosing) to indicate progress of each skill. Use the *Notes* section to record any observations or concerns. This chart can also be used to record pretest and posttest scores.

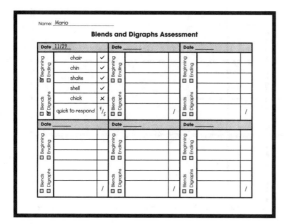

Use this page to asses each student's knowledge of blending sounds. Before the assessment, choose words specific to each skill and write or type them on index cards. Record the words used for the assessment in the first column. As you present each student with words, record how he performed with each word in the appropriate space on the chart using a check mark system. Record the total score at the bottom. Use the blank space at the bottom of each section to record any additional observations.

This page allows students to track their progress in recognizing and using consonant blends and digraphs. As each blend or digraph sound is mastered, the student should write the blend or digraph on a lily pad and then color it. Use the pond to record the date that the student mastered all blends or digraphs, or use it to record additional mastered blends and digraphs.

Blends and Digraphs Class Proficiency

Student Name	Blends		Digraphs		Notes
	Beginning	Ending	Beginning	Ending	

Blends and Digraphs Assessment

Name: _____

Date _____						/
☐ Beginning ☐ Ending						
☐ Blends ☐ Digraphs						

Date _____						/
☐ Beginning ☐ Ending						
☐ Blends ☐ Digraphs						

Date _____						/
☐ Beginning ☐ Ending						
☐ Blends ☐ Digraphs						

Date _____						/
☐ Beginning ☐ Ending						
☐ Blends ☐ Digraphs						

Date _____						/
☐ Beginning ☐ Ending						
☐ Blends ☐ Digraphs						

Date _____						/
☐ Beginning ☐ Ending						
☐ Blends ☐ Digraphs						

Name: _____

I Know Blends and Digraphs!

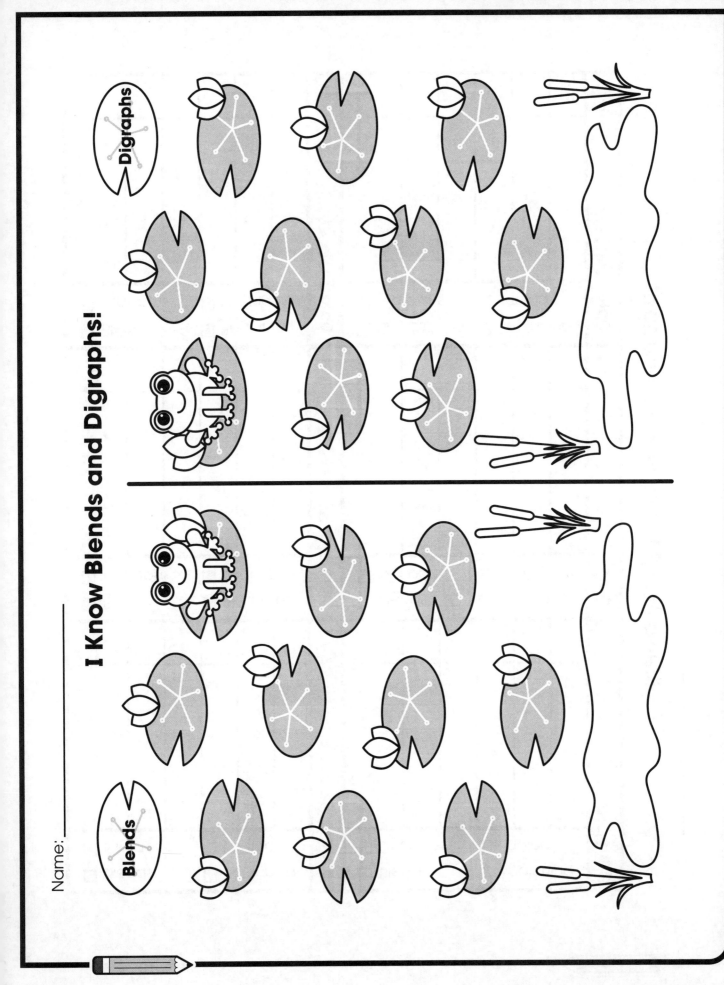

Digraphs

Blends

Syllables

This page is perfect for keeping a record of your class's proficiency with recognizing and decoding syllables in words. Record student names in the left-hand column. As you present the skills, record the date and skill level (note the scoring guide at the top of the page) to indicate the progress of each skill. Use the blank space at the bottom of each section to record any notes or concerns.

This page can be used to assess a student's progress in recognizing syllables in words. There is space for five words that have one syllable and five words that have two syllables. You can write these words on the board, allowing students to copy the words into the correct columns or you can say the words aloud and have students put a check mark in the correct column. More advanced students may also divide the two-syllable words into parts. Allow the student to record his score at the bottom of the form.

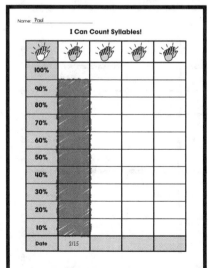

Students should keep this page to graph their scores on each syllable assessment. Students should record the date and graph the score of their assessment. This is a great form to present at parent-teacher conferences to show progression or mastery of syllable recognition.

Syllables Class Proficiency

☑ Observed ☒ Prompted

Student Name	Decodes one-syllable words			Decodes two-syllable words			Knows number of syllables in words by counting vowel sounds		

Syllables

Name _____ Date _____

One Syllable	Two Syllables
_____	_____
_____	_____
_____	_____
_____	_____
_____	_____

I got _____ out of _____ correct!

Syllables

Name _____ Date _____

One Syllable	Two Syllables
_____	_____
_____	_____
_____	_____
_____	_____
_____	_____

I got _____ out of _____ correct!

Name: _____

I Can Count Syllables!

👏	👏	👏	👏	👏
100%				
90%				
80%				
70%				
60%				
50%				
40%				
30%				
20%				
10%				
Date				

Spelling

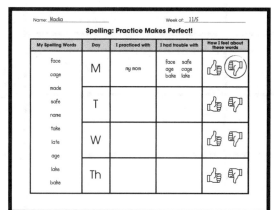

Spelling Class Proficiency

Week of __10/2__

Student Name	Score	Mostly random letters	Mostly phonetic	Mostly conventional	Notes
Owen	10/10			✓	
Marisa	5/10		✓		Only five words this week
	/				
	/				
	/				
	/				
	/				
	/				
	/				
	/				
	/				
	/				

(Stage columns are grouped under the heading "Stage")

This is an ideal page for recording scores of weekly spelling tests and at what spelling stage each student is performing. Record each student's name in the left-hand column. In the first column, record the score. You can use the divided space to record a pretest and posttest, the amount correct out of the total, or a date and the score. Make note of at what stage the student is at in his spelling skills by checking the appropriate column to the right. Use the *Notes* section to list any concerns or observations.

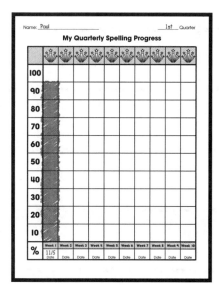

Name: __Nadia__   Week of: __11/5__

Spelling: Practice Makes Perfect!

My Spelling Words	Day	I practiced with	I had trouble with	How I feel about these words
face, cage, made	M	my mom	face safe age cage bake lake	👍 👎
safe, name	T			👍 👎
take, late, age	W			👍 👎
lake, bake	Th			👍 👎

Use this page for students' weekly spelling practice at home. At the beginning of the week, students should write their spelling words in the left-hand column. Each day, students will practice their words with a friend or family member and record the words they had trouble with. Then, students should record how they felt about their spelling practice by circling the thumbs-up or thumbs-down.

Name: __Paul__   __1st__ Quarter

My Quarterly Spelling Progress

%	Week 1 11/5 Date	Week 2 Date	Week 3 Date	Week 4 Date	Week 5 Date	Week 6 Date	Week 7 Date	Week 8 Date	Week 9 Date	Week 10 Date
100										
90										
80										
70										
60										
50										
40										
30										
20										
10										

This page highlights a student's spelling progress across 10 weeks or one quarter. It is a simple sheet that students can fill out themselves after they get their spelling test scores. For the purpose of this graph, convert their scores into percentages if this is not your usual way of grading. Regularly check in with students to see how they feel about their progress. This page allows you to troubleshoot if you notice a sudden dip in scores.

Spelling Class Proficiency

Week of _____

Student Name	Score	Stage			Notes
		Mostly random letters	Mostly phonetic	Mostly conventional	
	/				
	/				
	/				
	/				
	/				
	/				
	/				
	/				
	/				
	/				
	/				
	/				

Name: _____

Week of: _____

Spelling: Practice Makes Perfect!

My Spelling Words	Day	I practiced with	I had trouble with	How I feel about these words
	M			
	T			
	W			
	Th			

My Quarterly Spelling Progress

100										
90										
80										
70										
60										
50										
40										
30										
20										
10										
%	Week 1	Week 2	Week 3	Week 4	Week 5	Week 6	Week 7	Week 8	Week 9	Week 10
	Date	Date	Date	Date	Date	Date	Date	Date	Date	Date

Sight Words

Use this page to record sight word assessment scores for the entire class. After each assessment, record the date and the student's score. Use the blank space in each section to record any additional notes or observations.

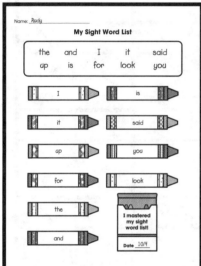

This page offers students a chance to prove mastery of new sight words. Have each student read his sight word list for the week aloud and then write each word in a crayon if they can read it correctly. At the end of the week, or when he masters the sight word list, the student should write the date in the crayon box.

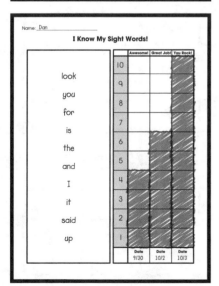

This page allows the student to highlight her progress with a set of sight words three times, such as pretest, practice, and posttest. Present a list of 10 sight words. The student should copy the list of words in the blank section. Then, have the student graph the number of sight words she reads correctly on each specified date.

Sight Words Class Proficiency

Student Name	Date	Score	Date	Score	Date	Score	Date	Score
		/		/		/		/
		/		/		/		/
		/		/		/		/
		/		/		/		/
		/		/		/		/
		/		/		/		/
		/		/		/		/
		/		/		/		/
		/		/		/		/

Name: _____

My Sight Word List

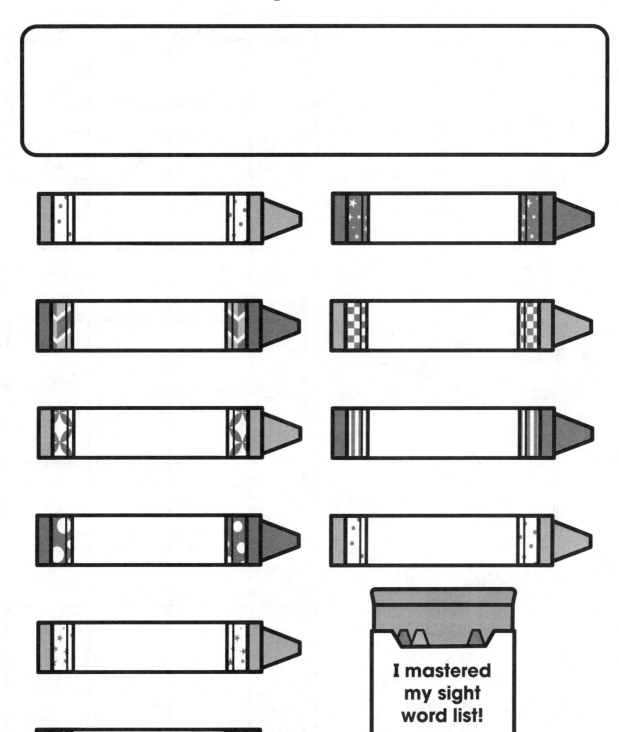

I mastered
my sight
word list!

Date _____

Name: _____

I Know My Sight Words!

	Awesome!	Great Job!	You Rock!
10			
9			
8			
7			
6			
5			
4			
3			
2			
1			
	Date	Date	Date

Fluency

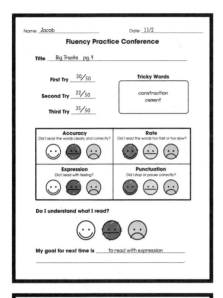

This page allows the student to rate his progress in the four main elements of oral fluency: expression, rate, punctuation, and accuracy. Present the student with a short passage to read. For each time the student reads the passage, record the number of words that he reads correctly. Record any tricky words that the student struggled with. Then for each element, the student should color a corresponding face to express how he felt about his fluency practice. The student should color how he felt about his comprehension of the passage and set a goal for the next time he reads for fluency practice.

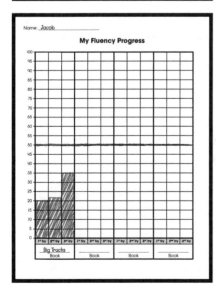

This page allows you to pinpoint progress for each student in the area of oral fluency. Give a student a short passage to read on four different occasions. Record the student's name in the left-hand column. Record the date and the fluency score each of the four times a student reads the passage. Problem words can also be noted. Use the *Notes* section to record any observations. Use the four ratings for each student to assess the overall level of progress (or lack of progress) with oral fluency.

This page allows students to track their own progress in reading fluently. For each practice, write the name of the book. Draw a line to represent the total number of words read in each passage. Then, record the number of words read correctly each time by coloring in the bar graph. It is recommended that you use a different color for each try to easily see progress in the same book.

Name: _____   Date: _____

Fluency Practice Conference

Title _____

First Try _____/_____

Second Try _____/_____

Third Try _____/_____

Tricky Words

Accuracy	**Rate**
Did I read the words clearly and correctly?	Did I read the words too fast or too slow?
Expression	**Punctuation**
Did I read with feeling?	Did I stop or pause correctly?

Do I understand what I read?

My goal for next time is _____

_____.

Fluency Practice Assessment

Name

	☐ /	**Notes**		☐ /	**Notes**
	Problem words			**Problem words**	
	☐ /	**Notes**		☐ /	**Notes**
	Problem words			**Problem words**	
	☐ /	**Notes**		☐ /	**Notes**
	Problem words			**Problem words**	
	☐ /	**Notes**		☐ /	**Notes**
	Problem words			**Problem words**	
	☐ /	**Notes**		☐ /	**Notes**
	Problem words			**Problem words**	
	☐ /	**Notes**		☐ /	**Notes**
	Problem words			**Problem words**	

Name: _____

My Fluency Progress

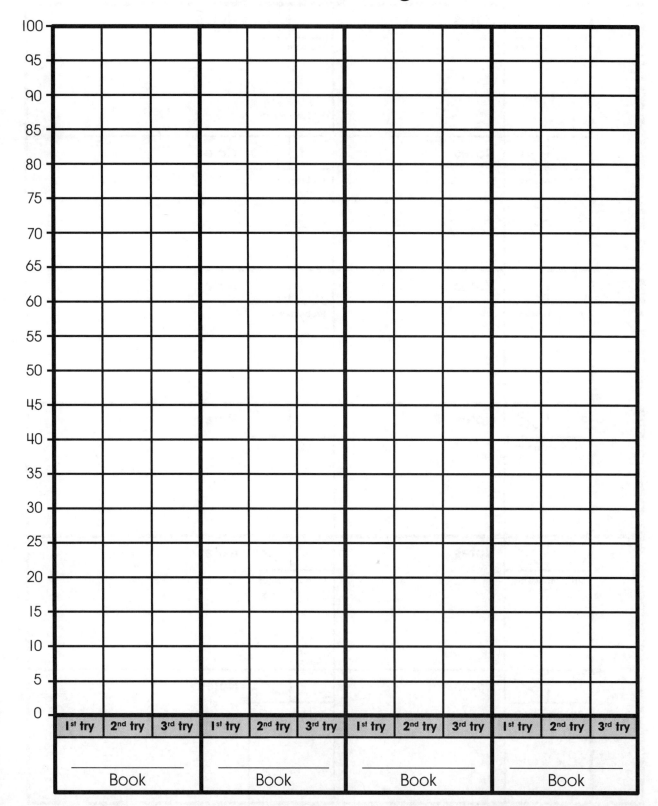

| | 1st try | 2nd try | 3rd try | 1st try | 2nd try | 3rd try | 1st try | 2nd try | 3rd try | 1st try | 2nd try | 3rd try |

_____   _____   _____   _____
      Book   Book   Book   Book

Writing
Standards Crosswalk

Kindergarten

Text Types and Purposes
- Use a combination of drawing, dictating, and writing to compose opinion pieces that tell a reader the topic or the name of the book they are writing about; state an opinion or preference about the topic or book.
- Use a combination of drawing, dictating, and writing to compose informative/explanatory texts that name what they are writing about and supply information about the topic.
- Use a combination of drawing, dictating, and writing to narrate a single event or several loosely linked events in the correct order, and provide a reaction to what happened.

Production and Distribution of Writing
With guidance and support:
- Respond to feedback from peers and add details to strengthen writing as needed.
- Explore a variety of digital tools to produce and publish writing, including in collaboration with peers.

Research to Build and Present Knowledge
- Participate in shared research and writing projects.
- With guidance and support, recall information from experiences or gather information from provided sources to answer a question.

Second Grade

Text Types and Purposes
- Write opinion pieces that introduce a topic or book, state an opinion, supply reasons to support the opinion, use linking words, and provide a concluding statement or section.
- Write informative/explanatory texts that introduce a topic, use facts and definitions to develop points, and provide a concluding statement or section.
- Write narratives that recount a well-elaborated event or short sequence of events; include details to describe actions, thoughts, and feelings; use temporal words to signal event order; and provide a sense of closure.

Production and Distribution of Writing
With guidance and support:
- Focus on a topic and strengthen writing as needed by revising and editing.
- Use a variety of digital tools to produce and publish writing, including in collaboration with peers.

Research to Build and Present Knowledge
- Participate in shared research and writing projects.
- Recall information from experiences or gather information from provided sources to answer a question.

Range of Writing (begins in grade 3)

Writing Concepts Checklist

Concept		Dates Taught				

Types of Writing

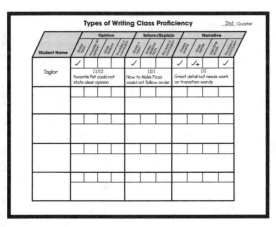

Each quarter, use this writing assessment checklist to keep track of each student's mastery of writing skills in each writing genre. As you introduce a skill, use a check mark rating system to record the proficiency of each skill. Use the blank space in each section to record notes or observations. Use this page to present information at principal-teacher or grade-level meetings.

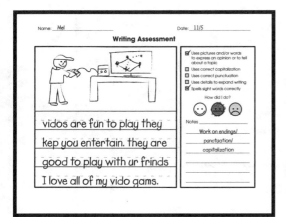

Use this page to guide a writing conference with each student. Have the student write a narrative, informational, or opinion piece. Use the checklist on the right to guide a writing conference with the student. Then, have the student color the face that best rates how she felt she did on the assessment. Make any observations in the *Notes* section. This is an excellent portfolio or parent-teacher conference piece.

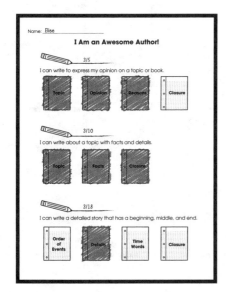

Use this page to allow students to take ownership of their writing skills. Each time a student masters a skill in each writing genre, he should color the piece of notebook paper with the skill listed. The student can write the date on the pencil line when all of the skills for a particular genre have been colored. Use this sheet to present at parent-teacher writing conferences to show writing progress.

Types of Writing Class Proficiency

Student Name	Opinion			Inform/Explain			Narrative			
	States topic	Provides an opinion	Gives reasons	Provides a conclusion	States a topic	States reasons/facts	Provides a conclusion	Orders events	Gives details	Uses time words	Provides a conclusion

Name: _____

Date: _____

Writing Assessment

Uses pictures and/or words to express an opinion or to tell about a topic

☐ Uses correct capitalization

☐ Uses correct punctuation

☐ Uses details to expand writing

☐ Spells sight words correctly

How did I do?

Notes _____

Name: _____

I Am an Awesome Author!

I can write to express my opinion on a topic or book.

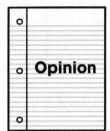

Topic   **Opinion**   **Reasons**   **Closure**

I can write about a topic with facts and details.

Topic   **Facts**   **Closure**

I can write a detailed story that has a beginning, middle, and end.

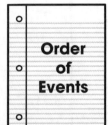

Order of Events   **Details**   **Time Words**   **Closure**

Improving Writing

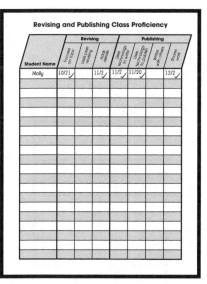

This page is perfect for seeing at a glance how your students are progressing in revising and publishing their written pieces. Use a date and check mark system to track each student's progress in improving their writing.

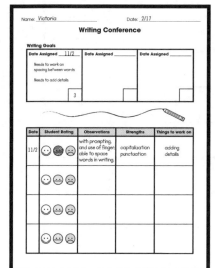

Use this page during student writing conferences about particular pieces of writing. Read the piece together and point out the good points and any errors. Then, conference with the student to assign writing goals. Write the date of the assignment. In each square, write the score of the writing piece that was assigned using a scale of your choosing. Note any goals that the student should focus on. In the bottom section, write the date and observations about the assigned writing. Add any strengths and goals for next time. Then, have the student rate his writing. If desired, attach the writing piece to the form or place the form at the beginning of a writing portfolio or folder.

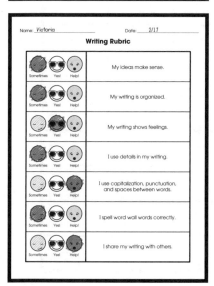

This page makes it easy for students to assess their own writing. After each writing assignment, students should color or circle a face to rate themselves on how well they have mastered each skill listed on the rubric. This form can also be introduced before the writing lesson to remind students of the skills they should use when writing.

Revising and Publishing Class Proficiency

Student Name	Revising			Publishing			
	Focuses on topic	Uses peer revising	Adds details	Uses technology to write	Uses technology to publish	Writes with others	Shares work

Name: _____

Writing Conference

Writing Goals

Date Assigned _____	Date Assigned _____	Date Assigned _____

Date	Student Rating	Observations	Strengths	Things to work on
	🙂 😐 🙁			
	🙂 😐 🙁			
	🙂 😐 🙁			
	🙂 😐 🙁			

Name: _____ Date: _____

Writing Rubric

 Sometimes Yes! Help!	My ideas make sense.
 Sometimes Yes! Help!	My writing is organized.
 Sometimes Yes! Help!	My writing shows feelings.
 Sometimes Yes! Help!	I use details in my writing.
 Sometimes Yes! Help!	I use capitalization, punctuation, and spaces between words.
 Sometimes Yes! Help!	I spell word wall words correctly.
 Sometimes Yes! Help!	I share my writing with others.

Speaking and Listening Standards Crosswalk

Kindergarten

Comprehension and Collaboration

- Participate in group discussions about grade-appropriate topics and texts.
- Follow agreed-upon discussion rules.
- Continue a conversation through multiple exchanges.
- Confirm understanding of a text or other information presented orally or through other media by asking and answering questions about key details and requesting clarification if needed.

Presentation of Knowledge and Ideas

- Describe familiar people, places, things, and events; with prompting and support, provide additional detail.
- Add drawings or visual displays to descriptions to provide additional detail.
- Speak audibly and express thoughts, feelings, and ideas clearly.

Second Grade

Comprehension and Collaboration

- Participate in group discussions about grade-appropriate topics and texts.
- Follow agreed-upon discussion rules.
- Comment on the remarks of others, and ask for clarification if needed.
- Recount or describe key ideas or details from a text or other channels of information.
- Ask and answer questions about a presentation to clarify comprehension, gather more information, or deepen understanding.

Presentation of Knowledge and Ideas

- Audibly and coherently tell a story or recount an experience with appropriate facts and relevant, descriptive details.
- Create audio recordings of stories or poems.
- Add drawings or other visual displays when appropriate.
- Produce complete sentences to provide requested detail or clarification.

Speaking and Listening Concepts Checklist

Concept		Dates Taught				

126 © Carson-Dellosa • CD-104917

Speaking and Listening Skills

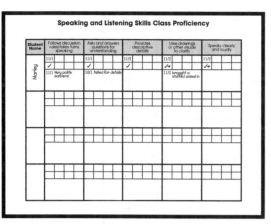

Use this page to keep track of your class's proficiency with speaking and listening skills. Record student names in the left-hand column. Each time students are assessed on a particular skill, use a check mark system to record their proficiency in that skill for the date observed. Make any notes or observations in the blank space in each section.

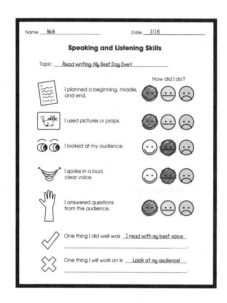

Use this page to help students self-assess their performance in a discussion or presentation. Students should color a face to rate how they felt they did in each skill area during the discussion or presentation. Have students record a strength and a goal for next time at the bottom of the page.

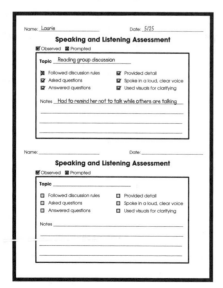

Use this page during individual conferences to give feedback to students after a presentation or discussion. Note the date and the topic of the discussion or presentation. Use the check boxes to assess each skill in speaking and listening (note the key at the top of the page). Record any notes or observations in the *Notes* section.

Speaking and Listening Skills Class Proficiency

Student Name	Follows discussion rules/takes turns speaking	Asks and answers questions for understanding	Provides descriptive details	Uses drawings or other visuals to clarify	Speaks clearly and loudly

Name: _____   Date: _____

Speaking and Listening Skills

Topic _____

How did I do?

 I planned a beginning, middle, and end.　

 I used pictures or props.　

 I looked at my audience.　

 I spoke in a loud, clear voice.　

 I answered questions from the audience.　

 One thing I did well was _____

_____.

 One thing I will work on is _____

_____.

Name: _____   Date: _____

Speaking and Listening Assessment

☑ Observed   ☒ Prompted

Topic _____

- ☐ Followed discussion rules   ☐ Provided detail
- ☐ Asked questions   ☐ Spoke in a loud, clear voice
- ☐ Answered questions   ☐ Used visuals for clarifying

Notes _____

_____

_____

_____

Name: _____   Date: _____

Speaking and Listening Assessment

☑ Observed   ☒ Prompted

Topic _____

- ☐ Followed discussion rules   ☐ Provided detail
- ☐ Asked questions   ☐ Spoke in a loud, clear voice
- ☐ Answered questions   ☐ Used visuals for clarifying

Notes _____

_____

_____

_____

Language
Standards Crosswalk

Kindergarten

Conventions of Standard English
- Print many upper- and lowercase letters.
- Use frequently occurring nouns and verbs; form regular plural nouns orally by adding *s* or *es*; understand and use question words; use the most frequently occurring prepositions.
- Produce and expand complete sentences in shared language activities.
- Capitalize the first word in a sentence; capitalize the pronoun *I*; recognize and name end punctuation.
- Write a letter or letters for most consonant and short-vowel sounds; spell simple words phonetically.

Knowledge of Language (Begins in grade 2)

Vocabulary Acquisition and Use
- Identify new meanings for familiar words.
- Use inflections and affixes as clues to word meaning.
- Sort common objects into categories.
- Relate frequently occurring verbs and adjectives to their opposites.
- Identify real-world connections between words and their use.
- Distinguish shades of meaning among similar verbs by acting them out.
- Use words and phrases acquired through conversations, reading and being read to, and responding to texts.

Second Grade

Conventions of Standard English
- Use collective nouns; form and use frequently occurring irregular plural nouns; use reflexive pronouns; form and use the past tense of common irregular verbs; use adjectives and adverbs appropriately.
- Produce, expand, and rearrange complete simple and compound sentences.
- Capitalize holidays, product names, and geographic names; use commas in greetings and closings of letters; use apostrophes to form contractions and frequently occurring possessives.
- Generalize learned spelling patterns when writing words; consult reference materials as needed to check and correct spellings.

Knowledge of Language
- Compare formal and informal uses of English.

Vocabulary Acquisition and Use
- Use sentence-level context as a clue to the meaning of a word or phrase.
- Determine meaning when a known prefix is added to a known word; use a known root word to determine an unknown word with the same root; use knowledge of individual words to predict the meaning of compound words; use glossaries and dictionaries to determine the meaning of new words.
- Identify real-world connections between words and their uses.
- Distinguish shades of meaning among related verbs and related adjectives.
- Use words and phrases (including descriptive adjectives and adverbs) acquired through conversations, reading and being read to, and responding to texts.

Language Concepts Checklist

Concept		Dates Taught			

Nouns and Pronouns

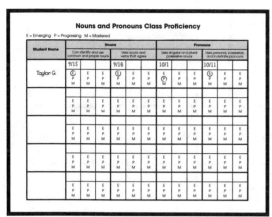

Use this page to track your class's proficiency levels in recognizing and using nouns and pronouns. Record student names in the left-hand column. As you assess the skills, record the date and circle *E*, *P*, or *M* (see the rating scale at the top of the page) to indicate the progress of each skill. This will allow you to see at a glance which students have mastered each skill and which students need more help.

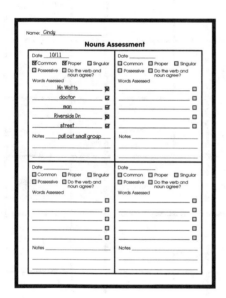

This one-on-one assessment page provides each student with the opportunity to show you what he knows about various types of nouns. Write the name of the student you are assessing and the date. Place a check mark by the type of nouns you are assessing. Then, present five words in the noun category you are assessing. You or the student can write the words in the spaces provided. Place a check mark in the boxes beside the nouns the student was able to identify or write correctly and an *X* beside the nouns that were incorrectly identified.

This interactive page allows students to track their knowledge of pronouns. As students are independently reading or in a small reading group setting, each student should write pronouns in the correct categories as she comes across them in her reading. After the student has found three pronouns in a category and correctly identified them, she should write the date at the bottom of the ice-cream cone.

Nouns and Pronouns Class Proficiency

E = Emerging P = Progressing M = Mastered

Student Name	Nouns						Pronouns					
	Can identify and use common and proper nouns			Uses nouns and verbs that agree			Uses singular and plural possessive nouns			Uses personal, possessive, and indefinite pronouns		
	E P M	E P M	E P M	E P M	E P M	E P M	E P M	E P M	E P M	E P M	E P M	E P M
	E P M	E P M	E P M	E P M	E P M	E P M	E P M	E P M	E P M	E P M	E P M	E P M
	E P M	E P M	E P M	E P M	E P M	E P M	E P M	E P M	E P M	E P M	E P M	E P M
	E P M	E P M	E P M	E P M	E P M	E P M	E P M	E P M	E P M	E P M	E P M	E P M
	E P M	E P M	E P M	E P M	E P M	E P M	E P M	E P M	E P M	E P M	E P M	E P M

Name: _____

Nouns Assessment

Date _____

☐ Common   ☐ Proper   ☐ Singular
☐ Possessive   ☐ Do the verb and noun agree?

Words Assessed

_____ ☐
_____ ☐
_____ ☐
_____ ☐
_____ ☐

Notes _____

_____

_____

Date _____

☐ Common   ☐ Proper   ☐ Singular
☐ Possessive   ☐ Do the verb and noun agree?

Words Assessed

_____ ☐
_____ ☐
_____ ☐
_____ ☐
_____ ☐

Notes _____

_____

_____

Date _____

☐ Common   ☐ Proper   ☐ Singular
☐ Possessive   ☐ Do the verb and noun agree?

Words Assessed

_____ ☐
_____ ☐
_____ ☐
_____ ☐
_____ ☐

Notes _____

_____

_____

Date _____

☐ Common   ☐ Proper   ☐ Singular
☐ Possessive   ☐ Do the verb and noun agree?

Words Assessed

_____ ☐
_____ ☐
_____ ☐
_____ ☐
_____ ☐

Notes _____

_____

_____

Name: _____

I Know Pronouns!

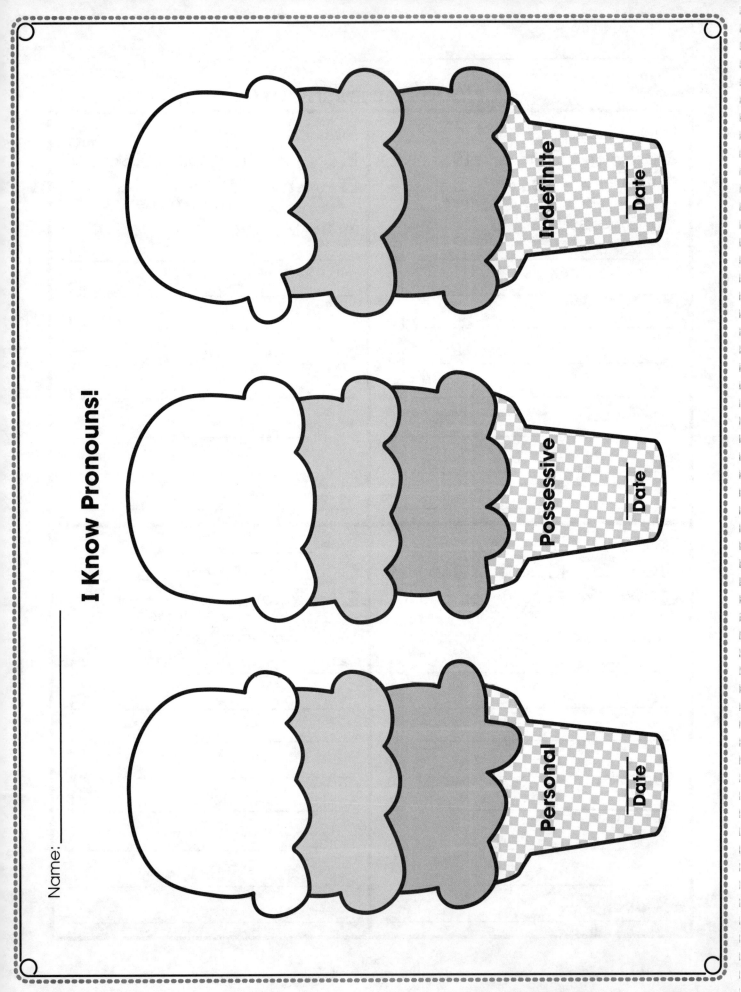

Personal

Date _____

Possessive

Date _____

Indefinite

Date _____

Verbs and Adjectives

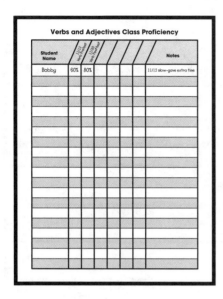

Use this page to track individual students' progress and proficiency with verbs and adjectives. Record student names in the left-hand column. As students are assessed, record the date and the score. Use the *Notes* section to record any additional observations. This sheet can also be used for pretest and posttest assessments.

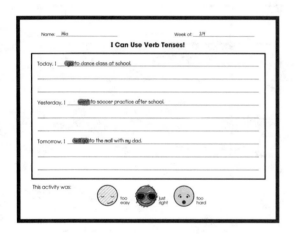

Use this page to assess students' understanding of verb tenses. The student should complete each sentence using the proper verb tense. Then, he should draw a box around or highlight the verb he used in each sentence. At the end of the assessment, he should rate how he felt about the activity by coloring one of the faces. This sheet makes an excellent portfolio tool to show proof of mastery or for parent-teacher conferences.

Use this page to assess students' understanding of using adjectives to describe. Each student should decide which object she will describe and then draw a picture of the object. She should then record adjectives that describe the object. At the end of the assessment, the student should rate how she felt about the activity by coloring one of the faces. Use the *Notes* section to record any observations. This page makes an excellent portfolio tool to show proof of mastery or for parent-teacher conferences.

Verbs and Adjectives Class Proficiency

Student Name							Notes

Name: _____   Date: _____

I Can Use Verb Tenses!

Today, I _____

_____

Yesterday, I _____

_____

Tomorrow, I _____

_____

This activity was:

too   just   too
easy   right   hard

Name: _____   Date: _____

I Can Use Adjectives!

I can describe _____ .

Words I can use

This activity was:

too easy   just right   too hard

Notes _____

_____

_____

140   © Carson-Dellosa • CD-104917

Prepositions

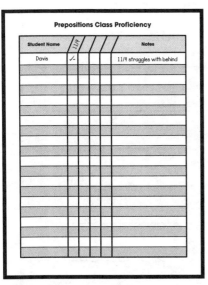

This page is useful for recording your class's proficiency in using prepositions. Record the preposition or other identifying information, such as test date, across the top. Use a check mark system or rating system of your choosing to record individual student proficiencies. Use the *Notes* column to record additional observations.

After introducing and practicing the concept of prepositions, allow students to show mastery of the concept with this page. The student should read each sentence and write an object in the first blank and a positional word or phrase in the second blank. (The last two sentences require a second object to fill in the third blank.) Then, the student should use the sentences she created to draw each object in the correct place in the picture. Finally, have the student color a face to show how she felt about the activity.

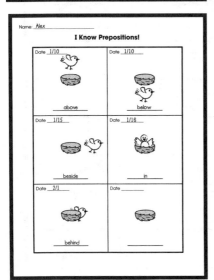

This page allows students to track their progress and take ownership of recognizing prepositions. As the student masters each preposition, he should write the date and the word. He should then draw a bird in the correct position near the nest to prove understanding of the preposition. Insert this page into a student's language arts portfolio to show proof of mastery.

Prepositions Class Proficiency

Student Name					Notes

Prepositions

A _____ is _____ the tree.

A _____ is _____ the cloud.

A _____ is _____ the bench.

A _____ is _____ the _____ .

A _____ is _____ the _____ .

This activity was:

too easy

just right

too hard

Name: _____

I Know Prepositions!

Date _____

Date _____

Date _____

Date _____

Date _____

Date _____

Capitalization and Punctuation

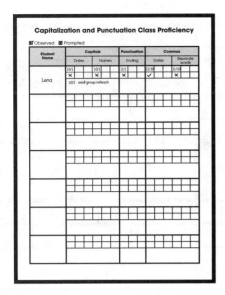

Use this page to track class proficiency levels in the skills of using correct capitalization and punctuation. Record student names in the left-hand column. As you assess the skills, record the date and a proficiency score (see the scoring guide at the top of the page) to indicate progress with each skill. Use the blank space in each section to record any notes or concerns. This will allow you to see at a glance which students have mastered each skill and which students need more help.

This page can be used to show proof of mastery with using correct capitalization as well as providing the student with a way to show pride in his progress. As a student masters writing a sentence with correct capitalization, allow him to demonstrate his knowledge by writing a sentence correctly in the corresponding section. Then, he should draw a box around or highlight each capital letter he used in the sentence. The student should also write the date he mastered each concept. Use this page in a portfolio to show mastery of correct capitalization.

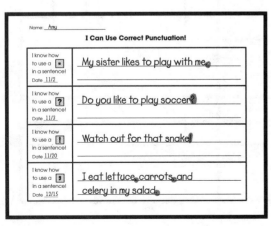

Allow students to show what they know in the skills of using correct punctuation. As a student masters writing a sentence with correct punctuation, allow her to demonstrate her knowledge by writing a sentence correctly in the corresponding section. Then, she should draw a box around or highlight each punctuation mark used in the sentence. The student should also write the date she mastered each concept. Use this page in a portfolio to show mastery of correct punctuation use.

Capitalization and Punctuation Class Proficiency

☑ Observed ☒ Prompted

Student Name	Capitals				Punctuation	Commas			
	Dates		Names		Ending	Dates		Separate words	

Name: _____

I Can Use Capital Letters!

Month Date _____	Day Date _____	Person Date _____	Pronoun Date _____

I Can Use Correct Punctuation!

Name: _____

I know how to use a **.** in a sentence! Date _____	
I know how to use a **?** in a sentence! Date _____	
I know how to use a **!** in a sentence! Date _____	
I know how to use a **,** in a sentence! Date _____	

Sentences

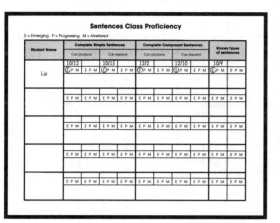

Use this sheet to track your class's proficiency levels with writing simple and compound sentences and their knowledge of the types of sentences. Record student names in the left-hand column. As the skills are assessed, record the date and circle *E*, *P*, or *M* (see the rating scale at the top of the page) to indicate the progress of each skill. Use the blank space at the bottom of each section to record notes or concerns. This will allow you to see at a glance which students have mastered each skill and which students need more help.

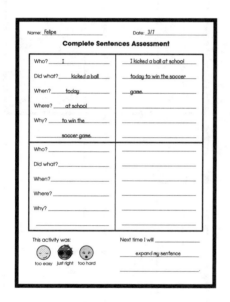

This form is the perfect tool for students to show proof of mastery for writing a complete sentence and the process that goes into it. Ask students to imagine a scenario, real or make-believe, and then write answers to the five *W*s. On the right side of the page, the student should use the words from the five *W*s activity to write a complete sentence. After giving students feedback on the successes or challenges of the first sentence, have students try again in the bottom section. Finally, ask students to rate the activity by coloring a face and to set a goal for improving their sentences next time.

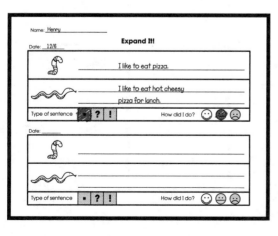

This page can be used in a one-on-one or small-group setting. First, have the student write a simple sentence on the top line. Then, conference with the student on how he can expand the sentence to add more detail. Allow the student to use his ideas to expand the first sentence and write the new sentence on the next set of lines. Next, have the student color the type of sentence he wrote. Finally, have the student color the appropriate face to show how he felt he did on the activity.

Sentences Class Proficiency

E = Emerging   P = Progressing   M = Mastered

Student Name	Complete Simple Sentences				Complete Compound Sentences				Knows types of sentences	
	Can produce		Can expand		Can produce		Can expand			
	E P M	E P M	E P M	E P M	E P M	E P M	E P M	E P M	E P M	E P M
	E P M	E P M	E P M	E P M	E P M	E P M	E P M	E P M	E P M	E P M
	E P M	E P M	E P M	E P M	E P M	E P M	E P M	E P M	E P M	E P M
	E P M	E P M	E P M	E P M	E P M	E P M	E P M	E P M	E P M	E P M
	E P M	E P M	E P M	E P M	E P M	E P M	E P M	E P M	E P M	E P M

Name: _____   Date: _____

Complete Sentences Assessment

Who? _____   _____

Did what? _____   _____

When? _____   _____

Where? _____   _____

Why? _____   _____

_____   _____

Who? _____   _____

Did what? _____   _____

When? _____   _____

Where? _____   _____

Why? _____   _____

_____   _____

This activity was:

too easy

just right

too hard

Next time I will _____

_____

_____.

Expand It!

Name: _____

Date: _____

How did I do?

| Type of sentence | . | ? | ! |

Date: _____

How did I do?

| Type of sentence | . | ? | ! |

Word Meanings

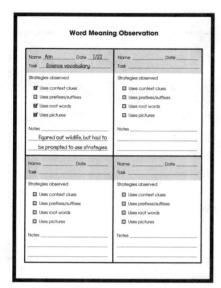

Use this page to informally assess individual students as you observe them individually or in a small reading group. As you observe a student during a vocabulary assignment, record the student's name, the date, the task assigned, and any word meaning strategies you observe the student using. Use the *Notes* section to record strengths and areas to focus on as well as specific observations. If desired, print this page on adhesive label sheets to keep on a clipboard (visit our website for a free downloadable template). This makes conferencing and moving logs to student folders quick and easy.

This page is useful in tracking students' vocabulary progress as they grow as readers. It can be used in a conference with individual students or in a small-group setting. When a student comes across a new word in her reading, she should write the word and the definition. She should also use the strategies at the top of the page to explain how she figured out the new word. The page gives you a quick look at a student's ability to use various strategies to learn new words.

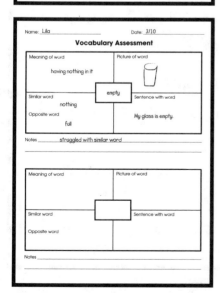

This page allows students to take ownership of figuring out unfamiliar words. The student should write the word in the center space, then write the meaning of the word. He may use any strategy to figure out the word's meaning. Once the student knows what the word means, have him draw a picture to represent it. Then, he should write the word's synonym and antonym and use it in a sentence. Use the *Notes* section to record any strengths or weaknesses you observed during the activity.

Word Meaning Observation

Name _____ Date _____

Task _____

Strategies observed

- ☐ Uses context clues
- ☐ Uses prefixes/suffixes
- ☐ Uses root words
- ☐ Uses pictures

Notes _____

_____

_____

Name _____ Date _____

Task _____

Strategies observed

- ☐ Uses context clues
- ☐ Uses prefixes/suffixes
- ☐ Uses root words
- ☐ Uses pictures

Notes _____

_____

_____

Name _____ Date _____

Task _____

Strategies observed

- ☐ Uses context clues
- ☐ Uses prefixes/suffixes
- ☐ Uses root words
- ☐ Uses pictures

Notes _____

_____

_____

Name _____ Date _____

Task _____

Strategies observed

- ☐ Uses context clues
- ☐ Uses prefixes/suffixes
- ☐ Uses root words
- ☐ Uses pictures

Notes _____

_____

_____

Name: _____

I Can Figure Out New Words!

Strategies > Context > Root Word > Word Parts > Pictures

Date _____

New Word _____

Definition _____

How I figured it out _____

_____

_____

Date _____

New Word _____

Definition _____

How I figured it out _____

_____

_____

Date _____

New Word _____

Definition _____

How I figured it out _____

_____

_____

Name: _____ Date: _____

Vocabulary Assessment

Meaning of word	Picture of word
Similar word	Sentence with word
Opposite word	

Notes _____

_____

Meaning of word	Picture of word
Similar word	Sentence with word
Opposite word	

Notes _____

_____

Word Relationships

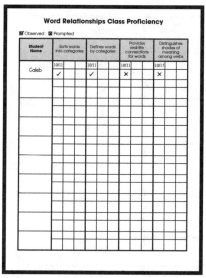

Use this page to track class proficiency levels in the skills of understanding word relationships. Record student names in the left-hand column. As the skills are assessed, record the date and a proficiency score (see the scoring guide at the top of the page) to indicate progress with each skill. This will allow you to see at a glance which students have mastered each skill and which students need more help.

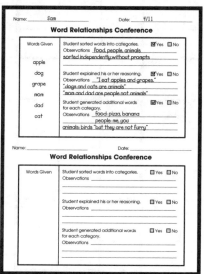

This page will make it easy to note a student's level of progress in understanding word relationships. In a one-on-one conference, provide the student with several words or picture cards to sort into categories. Write the words used in the left-hand column. Check off the boxes on the right side of the page as they apply. Also note any observations, such as how the student sorted the words or pictures and explained her reasoning. This form can also be used as proof of mastery to insert into a student's language arts portfolio.

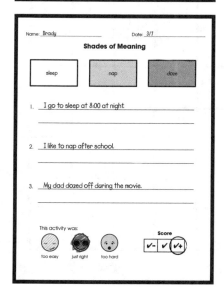

This page can be used to show proof of mastery of identifying shades of meaning between verbs. Provide a verb to the student and have him write it in the box. Then, the student should think of two more verbs that are similar to the first verb and write them in the next two boxes. The student should prove he knows the correct meaning by using each verb in a complete sentence. Have the student rate the activity by coloring a corresponding face at the bottom of the page. Circle or color a check mark to rate the student's work.

Word Relationships Class Proficiency

☑ Observed   ☒ Prompted

Student Name	Sorts words into categories			Defines words by categories			Provides real-life connections for words			Distinguishes shades of meaning among verbs		

Name: _____   Date: _____

Word Relationships Conference

Words Given	Student sorted words into categories.	☐ Yes ☐ No
	Observations _____	
	_____	
	_____	
	Student explained his or her reasoning.	☐ Yes ☐ No
	Observations _____	
	_____	
	_____	
	Student generated additional words for each category.	☐ Yes ☐ No
	Observations _____	
	_____	
	_____	

Name: _____   Date: _____

Word Relationships Conference

Words Given	Student sorted words into categories.	☐ Yes ☐ No
	Observations _____	
	_____	
	_____	
	Student explained his or her reasoning.	☐ Yes ☐ No
	Observations _____	
	_____	
	_____	
	Student generated additional words for each category.	☐ Yes ☐ No
	Observations _____	
	_____	
	_____	

Shades of Meaning

1. _____

_____

2. _____

_____

3. _____

_____

This activity was:

too easy

just right

too hard

Score

✔−	✔	✔+